BEYOND POVERTY AND THE WITCH HUNT

BEYOND POVERTY AND THE WITCH HUNT

THE SEARCH FOR MY MOTHER'S TRUTH

John Manneh

The following is the author's personal story,
accurate to the best of his recollection and understanding of facts
at the time. Some sequences, names, and identifying characteristics
have been changed to protect the privacy of individuals.

First edition, 2026

Cover and book design by Spring Cedars
Cover photo adapted from Radosław Botev,
Gambissara Gambia lumo, February 2007

ISBN 978-1-963117-95-0 (paperback)
ISBN 978-1-963117-96-7 (hardcover)
ISBN 978-1-963117-97-4 (ebook)

Published by Spring Cedars
Denver, Colorado
www.springcedars.com

CONTENTS

AUTHOR'S NOTE

This is a real story, told as truthfully as my memory allows.

The names and identifying details of most individuals mentioned in this memoir have been changed or omitted to protect their privacy. A number of characters are composites of people who played similar roles in my life. Some conversations have been reconstructed from memory and are not verbatim transcripts, but reflect the substance and spirit of what was said and felt. Certain events have been compressed or reordered to serve the flow of the narrative.

Memory is imperfect—especially memory formed in childhood, shaped by emotion and revisited across decades. Others who lived through these events alongside me may remember them differently, and I respect that. What I have written reflects my own experience, my own understanding, and my own truth.

This memoir was written out of love—for my mother, for my family, and for everyone who may think it is too late to learn their real story. It is never too late.

CHAPTER ONE

Many evenings during my early childhood in The Gambia, I would sprint toward my father the moment he arrived home after a long day at work, a beaming smile crinkling at the corners of his eyes. My father lifted me effortlessly, and I laughed. He was a large man, and I was small enough for him to toss me playfully into the air.

My older brothers, Jose and Patrick, were my protectors, armed with banter and the occasional piece of sage advice. They taught me how to hunt and raise animals like goats; they shared secrets with me and offered camaraderie that deepened my happiness.

I had a third brother, Greg, who was years older than Jose and Patrick. Greg didn't live with us anymore, but he often visited. His presence was kind and gentle, with a carefree spirit that made our interactions feel lighthearted.

I remember one morning, the sun peeked over the horizon,

casting a warm golden glow that enveloped our village like a soft blanket. As Patrick and I went outside, our loyal dog, Napoleon, bounded ahead, his tail wagging with excitement, leading us into the lush, green bush that surrounded our home.

"Remember, John, patience is key," Patrick whispered to me, his voice low and measured as we wove our way through the thick undergrowth, our eyes darting between the leaves, searching for any flicker of movement.

Suddenly, Napoleon's ears perked up at a sound. With a burst of energy, he dashed forward, disappearing into a tangle of bushes. Moments later, he emerged, clutching a bush rat in his jaws, his eyes gleaming with triumph. Patrick's face broke into a wide grin as he knelt down to ruffle Napoleon's fur. "Good boy!" he said.

As dusk settled, we gathered around a crackling campfire, the aroma of roasting bush rat wafting through the air.

"Today is a good day," Patrick said, as we savored our hard-earned meal. We exchanged tales of past escapades and spun dreams of adventures still to come.

Then we made our way to the river, its tranquil waters glimmering like glass under the brightening sun. Patrick took some sturdy rope and, with deft hands, tied it securely to a robust tree branch, fashioning a makeshift swing that hung over the water's edge. With a carefree laugh, I charged from the riverbank, the wind whipping through my hair as I soared through the air, feeling weightless, before plunging into the cool, refreshing water below.

Our final challenge of the day awaited us in the muddy riverbed, where elusive creatures scuttled about, their quick movements barely visible. Crouching, Patrick demonstrated the art of crab-catching, his hands deliberate. With his guidance, I soon grasped the technique, a rush of pride swelling in my chest as I held up my very first catch. The tiny crab pinched at my fingers.

As the sun dipped below the horizon, painting the sky with vibrant shades of orange and pink, we made our way home. The experiences we shared had become an inseparable part of our friendship. Not only had Patrick been my partner in these adventures, but he had also become a mentor, imparting valuable lessons and nurturing my spirit with every step we took together in the wild.

In the early mornings, my older brothers and I bundled up against the chilly bite of the air and set out on our little adventures to gather weeds and sticks with my father. The ground was slightly frosted, and our breath formed visible puffs in the crisp atmosphere. We prepared to build a fire to keep warm. While we worked side by side, my father shared amusing anecdotes and silly jokes from his youth, his voice full of nostalgia and mischief.

As we wandered through the dew-kissed fields in search of kindling, my father, whom I called Baba, began one of his entertaining tales. "Did I ever tell you about the time, John, when I tried to outrun a chicken?" he asked me.

"No, Baba! What happened?" I leaned in, eager to hear.

"Once, when I was young, I challenged the neighbor's rooster to a race. I took off like a shot, but that rooster was quick. Just as I thought I was winning, I tripped and fell into the cold river!"

We burst into laughter.

"What happened next?"

"The rooster strutted away in victory while I waded home, soaked and humiliated. That day, I learned never to underestimate a hungry rooster!" Baba said. "Now, back to finding those sticks!"

Though my father rarely drank, he would have a glass here and there. Once, after a few sips of whisky, he put the glass down and belted out his favorite song. I knew what was coming next, and I inched a bit closer to him, a grin stretching across my face. He would take another sip or two, and I would wait for him to turn to me and reach for my hand.

"Let's dance!" he said. With our fingers clasped together, we skipped around the table as his booming voice filled our tiny living room. His palm felt warm against mine, and his long fingers wrapped around my tiny pinkie finger. When his song was over, we were both out of breath. He laughed and said, "Again?" and I responded, "Yes! Again!"

My mother, however, was the soft-spoken one in our family; her presence was serene and grounding. I called her Nteh, which means *mother* in my native language, but her given name was Mado. Every day, when Nteh went to the market, I sat on the porch, feeling a bubbling excitement in my chest as I awaited her return, hoping for a special treat. Soon, I saw her familiar figure approaching, a basket full of vibrant produce and fragrant spices balancing on her head. I rushed to greet her, my eyes drawn to the colorful array of ingredients that promised a delicious meal to come.

"Ah, my little one," Nteh said, her soft voice comforting after the day's adventures. However, before I could have my treat—whether it was sweet ice or fried dough—she asked me to help clean the fish and wash any dirty dishes. As we entered the small kitchen built next to the house, my mother began the rhythmic dance of preparing our meal, her skilled hands moving with grace and precision. I watched in wonder as she transformed the ingredients into a mouthwatering dish of tantalizing aromas. Nteh's dedication to nurturing our family bonds was steadfast.

Even with the moments of my childhood that were formative and grounding, there was a stark backdrop of poverty pressing down on my family. We were nestled in an impoverished African village, and each day was a struggle for survival against overwhelming odds.

Every morning, my eyes fluttered open to the sight of our mud block, a structure that had weathered countless storms and seasons. Its once-vibrant thatched roof now sagged under the assault of time and the unforgiving elements. My father, a man of remarkable resilience, dedicated himself to repairing that weary roof. At first, he would gather tufts of grass, weaving them into the crevices. As his financial condition gradually improved, he made the leap to corrugated roofing, an upgrade he took great pride in.

On the day Baba decided to replace the thatched roof with a corrugated one, the morning sun filtered through the thinning thatch, casting a patchwork of light. He had been toiling tirelessly, and today marked a turning point in our lives. I could sense the anticipation as my father beckoned us to gather outside our humble home.

"Today, our lives are changing!" Baba's eyes gleamed with a determination that I had come to admire over the years. Before us, a stack of corrugated roofing sheets stood as a testament to my father's resilience and pursuit of better circumstances. His hands, calloused from years of labor, carefully lifted the first sheet, aligning it with the edge of our mud house. One by one, we joined forces to secure each sheet, our hearts swelling with a profound sense of accomplishment. The resounding echoes of each clang and thud reverberated through the village, signaling a new era for our family. As the last sheet was put into place, our home transformed before our eyes, now boasting a roof that promised sturdier protection. In that moment, the long grip of poverty seemed to recede ever so slightly. Together, we had turned a dream into a reality, and our joy would fuel our spirits for the challenges yet to come.

Inside our modest home, the conversation surrounding food was often dominated by the scarcity that defined our daily reality. The mere mention of meat evoked feelings of longing, as it was regarded as an extravagant luxury, a prized delicacy reserved for occasions like Christmas and for when we had very important guests. On that singular day, my parents modified our living space into a scene of celebration. They prepared a lavish feast, a meal of meat that would be the highlight of our day or year, depending on the occasion.

In the days leading up to Christmas, there was a palpable buzz of excitement, accompanied by the melodious sounds of laughter and chatter throughout our home and the entire village. The joyous ambiance brought our family together, each of us eager for the arrival of the long-anticipated celebration. The day was magical, and I was so happy to receive a nice outfit from my parents and a flawless pair of shoes. My breath caught in my throat when I saw the shoes. The deep and inviting hue of the leather and delicate stitching made them appear luxurious.

"Go ahead, John, try them on!" my mother urged. Her eyes sparkled like stars as they mirrored my own excitement. I slipped my feet into the shoes, marveling at how they caressed my skin, hugging the contours of my feet in a perfect embrace. Standing tall in my new footwear, I felt an exhilarating sense of confidence washing over me. As I paraded around the living room, the rhythmic tapping of my shoes against the floor resonated with the cheerful applause of my family. These simple yet profound gestures pierced through the veil of our otherwise grim circumstances, granting us a fleeting taste of joy and normalcy amidst the struggles we faced.

But the money my family had for my new pair of shoes was just that—money for only one pair, and no money for anything else. Our poverty was so pervasive that I had no choice but to fashion plastic bags into a backpack. A sight all too common among the countless other children who shared our unfortunate situation.

My mother even repurposed discarded cooking oil containers as makeshift lotion, an attempt to salvage some semblance of comfort and dignity in a world that often felt harsh and unyielding.

My footsteps brushed along the dusty path leading to our home, and the weight of my bag against my back was a reminder of a day filled with adventure and growth. I approached our modest house and could see my parents' expectant faces; their expressions were of love and concern.

"Welcome home, my child," my mother greeted me. "Let's take care of those shoes, shall we?"

I nodded, understanding the importance of preserving my only pair of shoes. With care, I slipped them off, feeling the cool earth beneath my feet. A sense of relief washed over me when I placed them safely by the door, a symbolic gesture of gratitude for the small blessings in our lives. From that moment on, I decided to walk barefoot for the rest of the day.

Despite the poverty in our area of The Gambia, our home was a sanctuary overflowing with laughter and kindness, creating an atmosphere that made even the most daunting challenges seem surmountable.

One day, as the sun was setting and casting a golden glow over our small home, I remember we gathered in the living room, our eyes fixed on the steaming plates of food that my mother had prepared. Her ability to turn the simplest ingredients into a feast was nothing short of magic, filling our hearts with thankfulness and our bellies with warmth.

As we savored the flavors, my father leaned back in his chair. "Did I ever tell you about the time I came across a hyena on a road at night when I was still young in Guinea-Bissau?" he asked.

I shook my head, curiosity piqued by the promise of another captivating story. With each word, he painted a vivid picture of his youth, weaving in lessons of resilience and determination that lit up any dark corner.

"As I walked through the evening landscape, the air was thick with an eerie stillness that sent shivers down my spine. It was then that I first spotted a shadowy figure lurking in the underbush, my mind initially convincing me that it was a mere dog. Yet, I was careful to close the distance; the dim light revealed the unmistakable silhouette of a hyena, its lean body framed against the backdrop of tangled grass and darkened trees. A rush of adrenaline flooded my veins, igniting my instincts with primal fear. The creature's haunting laugh echoed in my memory, and I knew all too well the danger it posed. Without a second thought, I spun on my heels and sprinted back the way I came, my heart pounding like a drum in my chest. The once-familiar path seemed to twist and loom ominously before me, shadows lengthening as I raced toward the safety of home. A sense of urgency propelled me forward as the darkness closed in around me."

Laughter burst out, spilling from my lips. In these cherished moments, our home became a sanctuary of love and happiness. The gentle wisdom of our parents nourished our spirits. Our financial struggles, though always present, seemed to fade into the background, overshadowed by the strength and unity of our family. The deep love that bound us together was our armor against the harsh realities of poverty, transforming our humble home into a haven.

Though I had memories of a family that contained love, support, and resilience, there were times when my curiosity led to a deeper layer that my mother and father probably didn't want me to know about at such a young age. However, I always felt there was something else going on, something unspoken. I felt there was something no one was telling me directly.

Throughout my years, I had heard bits and pieces of

conversations, whispers, and murmurs, but my young brain couldn't connect all the dots together and get them to make sense.

I was about seven or eight when this unspoken truth began to dawn on me. On several occasions, I overheard my mother and father talking about Greg, and then distinctly heard them say the word *father*. I didn't quite know how or when my brain started to pick up on the pieces, but it did. I suppose my subconscious knew the truth before I did. But why would Baba, my father, talk to my mother about my older brother Greg and then say *father*? This confused me.

My parents were sitting in the kitchen, and I hid just around the corner. I heard them pour cups of tea and pictured them sitting in the wooden chairs.

"I always love it when he's here with us," Baba said. "This is Greg's home, and no matter how old he grows, he can always come back here. It's good for everyone."

"Well, what will we do if she wants to come visit again? Do you remember what happened last time she visited?" my mother asked.

I wondered who *she* was. And when was the time *she* visited? I didn't remember a visit from any woman.

"No one has heard from her for a long time," Baba said.

"Regardless, I think it's good for John to have his father in the house with him," my mother said.

My entire core shook.

"Yes, it is good for a son to have his father in the house."

Why would they say it like that, *it's good for a son to have his father in the house often?*

CHAPTER TWO

Greg, the person I had always known as my eldest brother, was, in fact, my biological father. This revelation unfolded quietly within me—no one in my family ever told me that Greg was my father. I just sort of put the pieces of the truth together and then continued to act like everything was okay. No one in the household had any idea what I had discovered on my own. I maintained the silence and continued with life as if nothing had changed. But the truth was overwhelming; this shocking realization made me more aware of the complexities of my family dynamics.

For all my years up to that point, I had comfortably called my eldest brother "Greg," a name that rolled off my tongue so easily, a name that felt familiar and safe. Yet now, the very utterance of his name had new emotional weight. I was bewildered, my heart racing as a storm of confusion, anger, and sadness surged within me.

Though Greg was always welcome at the house with no issues at all, he frequently disappeared into the distance, working in a town far beyond our village to ensure his financial stability. His intermittent presence in my life only deepened the emotional distance between us, turning my days into a series of unanswered questions and unfulfilled yearnings. Sometimes when he visited, we shared a quick embrace, a fleeting hug that barely masked his absences. In that brief moment of connection, I felt both comfort and longing.

Each visit of Greg's began in a different way, but my anticipation was the same. There were returns of his where I would see him coming down the road. The air was tense as I stood at the threshold of our home, watching the familiar silhouette of Greg—my father—draw nearer.

The sun dipped below the horizon, casting warm golden hues that danced across the ground, but my heart felt heavy. His long absences had carved out a void in our relationship, an aching chasm with unspoken words.

"Come here, John," he called, his voice soft, yet still bearing the fatigue of his weary travels. With each step I took toward him, the world around me faded into a blur. I nestled against him, and his strong arms wrapped around me, radiating a feeling of home. In that instant, the chaos of the outside world dissolved; it was just him and me, lost in a cocoon of familiarity and safety. Yet, buried within that sense of wholeness was a profound ache, a haunting reminder of the countless nights we had spent apart, each tick of the clock amplifying the distance that had grown between us and the questions that remained.

As our hug loosened, the harsh reality of our inevitable separation crept back in, splintering the fragile peace we had so briefly reclaimed. We savored this fleeting connection, so precious and precarious.

On some of his other visits, I would be in the house, not watching the road at all. I would hear the familiar creak of the door, a signal that sent my heart fluttering. As Greg stepped into the room, his presence filled the entire space. We exchanged smiles; the unspoken emotions hung heavy. As we gathered in the living room, our conversation remained polite, skimming the surface of deeper issues yet to be addressed.

"How was your journey?" Nteh asked.

"Tiring, but I'm glad to be home," my father answered.

While the world around me remained blissfully oblivious to the secret I carried deep within, I chose to cradle it close to my heart. This truth, like a silent storm brewing inside me, demanded my attention, yet I made every effort to maintain the delicate harmony of my life. I often recall Patrick's lighthearted personality; his laughter echoes in my thoughts to this day. After the revelation, however, I felt an inexplicable distance begin to grow wider each day, leaving me unsure of how to process my life and other relationships now that I knew the truth.

I lingered awkwardly in the corner. My family, oblivious to my unease, ate their meals and talked as they always had.

Patrick then called to me with concern and affection. "Hey, leave that post you are leaning on and come eat! This is your home; stop acting like a stranger in your father's house!" Patrick was referring to my grandfather. But now this word, this person, had an entirely new meaning in my head, and I struggled to fully grasp this meaning.

I constantly thought about the mystery that was my father. His presence was a blend of comfort and confusion, a reminder of both what I cherished and what eluded me. With each brief reunion, I was left with the unanswered questions, suspended, haunting me long after he had gone.

One night, we sat for dinner; the familiar dishes laid out created a warm atmosphere. My father's silhouette, framed by the fading light spilling through the window, cast long shadows across the bare floor. The comforting aroma of Nteh's stew wafted through the air. Though the meal was simplistic, there was an unspoken respect for the food before us; each ingredient represented a triumph over scarcity and a testament to our resourcefulness. These meals provided nourishment and the wonderful presence of loved ones gathered around the table. The flickering light of a single kerosene lamp danced upon our faces, illuminating the lines etched by hardship and joy. This was more than just a meal; it was a quiet ritual that bonded us and symbolized our perseverance through adversity. During the meal, our exchanges became a mosaic of fragmented thoughts and guarded feelings.

"Will you pass the pepper to me, John, please?" asked Patrick.

I passed it without saying a word.

"How was your day, Greg?" my mother asked.

"Oh, just fine, same as always," he answered. "Nothing new going on in my life."

I watched his face as his lips moved and his eyes locked on Nteh. I looked for glimpses of the man I knew he was—the father I wished to connect with more deeply. Yet his words always danced around the core of the matter.

He sat only two chairs away from me. The lack of open and truthful conversation within the family only intensified my longing. But speaking of such intimate matters was not customary in our culture.

We ate the rest of our meal in silence. When we finished, the conversation picked back up, polite and cautious, always skipping over the questions that burned in my heart. My father stood up to leave the table. As he walked behind me, he placed a hand on my shoulder. I turned my head to look up at him, and his eyes seemed to apologize. In that moment, I held onto the hope that someday we would find the words to close the gap between us, to weave the pieces of our bond into understanding and love.

Lying in bed later that night, I listened to the chirping crickets and rustling leaves. Their rhythm contrasted with the chaos that consumed my mind.

There was a singular time when Greg chastised me for wetting the bed. I had outgrown the habit, but ironically, it struck again during the weekend of his visit, catching me off guard in the quiet of the night. I stirred from sleep, and the telltale warmth beneath the sheets jolted me awake, filling me with embarrassment. Greg, typically a source of patience and gentle guidance, reacted with an expression of shock that I had never seen before. In a rare moment of frustration, he reached for his belt, the leather glinting ominously in the faint light of the room. "Why did you pee in bed, a big boy like you?" he asked, the disappointment in his voice cutting through the hazy remnants of my dreams.

I felt a rush of shame in that instant. It was the only time I can recall he ever resorted to such discipline. Always believing in gentle guidance over physical punishment, my father was soft-hearted and nurturing.

My fervent desire to uncover my family history deepened. I realized how my past was one layer within the larger workings of Gambian society, punctuated by injustices that left scars on both individuals and communities. This realization ignited a relentless quest within me to delve into the profound questions surrounding my origins and heritage.

I would soon find out that my own experiences were not isolated; rather, they echoed the stories of countless others who had traversed similar situations. The elusive nature of truth, often shrouded in layered memories, was at the center of my journey. The chasm between memory and reality required my careful examination and interpretation. I needed to unearth stories that would be both painful and enlightening.

Greg was indeed my father. But who exactly was my mother? What circumstances led to her absence in my life? This was a dark cloud looming over me, heavy and unyielding, creating a profound void that felt insurmountable. The ache gnawed at my spirit, leaving me longing for a connection I had never known. I decided I would ask my grandparents and uncles when an opportunity arose.

I vividly remember a quiet afternoon when I sat beside my grandfather under a mango tree. Eager and a little anxious, I turned to him and asked, "Baba, does anyone know where my mother is?"

His wise eyes, a reflection of many years filled with experience, grew big for just a moment, then softened as he looked down at me. He took a moment of silence before he replied, "Who told you, my dear boy? Who told you the truth about your mother and father?"

"No one did, Baba. I figured it out on my own."

"You are smart and so observant. But I will tell you right now, no one truly knows where your mother is. However, I have faith that she will come to visit us again one day." His voice, though tinged with sadness, held an undercurrent of hope, assuring me that I was not alone.

At some point after my conversation with Baba, he must have told Patrick, Jose, and my grandmother that I had figured out who my biological father was. And like a flame in a forest fire, moving quickly from one tree to another, one of them must have told Greg that I knew who he really was. But the fire stopped there. My family did not seem to see an urgency to offer me an explanation, because not one said a word to me about it. Everyone just moved on as if nothing had happened. In our culture, such matters were not discussed, especially with children. So I continued to struggle on my own.

Feelings of betrayal and loss filled every fiber of my being. One afternoon, I saw a mother embracing her children by the local soccer field, and a wrenching pang of longing shot through my heart. It must be nice to have your mother around. It struck deep within me, taking root, and I waited anxiously for the right moment for the feeling to dissolve into nothingness.

Amidst my emotional chaos, I found refuge in the resolute love and unwavering support of the people I now understood to be my grandparents. I knew I had to live with this new reality, and the ground beneath me felt unstable, yet I pressed forward with determination. I donned the mask of normalcy, projecting strength as if nothing had changed. During moments of perplexity, I took refuge in the profound bond I shared with my grandparents. They were the lighthouses in the tempest of my emotions, their love and wisdom radiating brightness that cut through the thick fog of confusion. I was not merely a grandchild, but rather a cherished piece of their very souls—a bond that transcended the traditional roles of a grandparent and grandson.

But as time unfurled, the trail to my mother's whereabouts grew ever fainter, her very existence becoming enveloped in a shroud of uncertainty. My grandparents' reassuring presence reminded me that family extended beyond mere genetic ties; it resided in the hearts that nurture, support, and cherish one another, providing a sanctuary amid life's challenges. But still, I wondered who my mother was, where she went, and most importantly, why.

CHAPTER THREE

Our family farmed a trio of staples—rice, beans, and cassava —with rice reigning as our primary crop. Its golden grains were not only a vital source of nourishment but also held cultural significance in our daily lives. Each dawn, as the first light pierced through the veil of night, Baba would nudge me awake. "Time to rise and shine; it's a big day at the farm!" he declared, urging me to greet the morning with purpose.

Before breakfast, I would venture outside with our bleating goats and set off to find the lush, green pastures nearby. The goats, with their playful antics, provided me with companionship as I led them through the fields. Throughout the day, my grandfather often reminded me to keep an eye on them. "Go check on the goats," he would say, ensuring they were content and safe.

However, the heart of our labor lay in the rice fields, which demanded immense dedication and effort. These fields sprawled far beyond our home, nestled in the fertile land that promised a rich harvest. My grandfather's calls would echo in my ears, rallying me for the arduous trek ahead. And again, the next day, it was: "Wake up! It's time to go to the farm!" Each step we took toward the fields served as a reminder of the fruits of our labor. Those days spent on the farm contained hard work, laughter, and unforgettable memories that I will always hold dear.

My grandparents frequently tasked Patrick and me with the important job of fetching water from a source near the airport, conveniently situated outside our fields. This chore quickly became one of our most cherished activities, offering us the rare chance to observe majestic planes soaring through the sky, gracefully touching down, or ascending into the clouds. Watching those powerful machines dance through the air filled us with awe and a sense of adventure.

Our escapades didn't stop there. I fondly recall our trips to the airport dumpsite, where we eagerly dug through the remnants left by travelers. It felt like a thrilling quest, hunting for treasures that others had discarded. We combed through the remains of meals, delighting in finding treats like cookies that still looked tempting. Each plastic spoon and fork added to our growing collection. In our resourceful scavenging, we also gathered hand wipes, which we used to freshen up, feeling almost luxurious amidst our playful exploration. The experience of rummaging through the trash was anything but mundane; it was thrilling, where each item felt like a prize, a trophy of our little quests.

One morning, my world changed once more. The sunlight spilled through the windows, bathing my room in a warm, golden light. It was the same sunlight that danced across Jose's face. But he was no longer my older brother; he was now Uncle to me, though I had yet to say it aloud. His smile was wide and infectious as he proclaimed, "Today, my boy, you start a brand-new chapter in your life!"

His enthusiasm resonated with me, causing my heart to swell with anticipation as we prepared for my very first day of school. Walking hand in hand with Jose toward the school, I felt the comforting grip of his calloused hand enveloping my small one, steady and reassuring. The air was crisp and fragrant with the sweet scent of blooming flowers, while the lively sounds of the village buzzed around us: the cheerful laughter of children, the rustling of leaves in the gentle breeze, and the faint melody of birds singing their morning songs. We passed clusters of children with bright, eager faces, hurrying by in their uniforms, the fabric crisp and tidy, and their satchels bouncing against their backs.

"You will learn a great many things here, my boy," Jose said. "But always remember that the values of our family and the timeless lessons of the land we come from will guide and sustain you." He paused to look deep into my eyes, then squeezed my hand before releasing it, a final gesture of encouragement and love. I felt a swirl of emotions, thrilling and daunting all at once. I crossed the threshold of the classroom, pushed on the heavy metal door, and took a deep breath, fully aware that my journey was about to begin. With Jose's support and guidance in my heart, I felt ready to face anything that lay ahead.

The school bell's chime resonated like a clarion call, heralding the arrival of students. Amid a sea of curious and unfamiliar faces, I experienced trepidation. That new chapter Jose told me about was beginning, promising endless possibilities, and although I was excited, a part of me ached for the farm. Those early morning wake-up calls were often a struggle, but as soon as I arrived in the field and began my work, any fatigue melted away, replaced by a sense of purpose and fulfillment.

That first day at school, I saw only one other child about my age in my class, a girl. Everyone else was a bit younger, probably seven, which was the average age to start school in The Gambia. I figured I was starting later because I lived on a farm and needed to help my family. While I wanted the girl to at least acknowledge me and give me some sort of signal that she knew she was my age, she didn't.

A boy approached me, his smile radiating kindness and openness. "Hello," he said. "What's your name? You are new here, no? Where do you live?"

He peppered me with so many questions that I could not answer them fast enough. But his greeting was so enthusiastic. I felt the first sparks of friendship igniting between us, and I marveled at the miraculous ease with which these strangers became allies in this vast and uncharted world.

Moments later, a teacher called out to our small group that had gathered. "Please line up," she said, and the children formed a neat line just outside the door. I stood there, not knowing where to go into the line: the front, the middle, or the back? Since I was new to this, I wasn't sure if each student had to stand in a certain place in the line.

"Psst. You go like this. Stand here," my new friend pointed in front of his toes. "You can be before me."

And so our neat line formed just outside the classroom door on my very first day of school, and this was to be my spot in line all year.

After circle time and reading, the comforting aroma of warm milk drifted out of the classroom. The room still had the scent of polish and cleaning supplies, but this new smell added a delightful promise of nourishment. Memories of many cozy afternoons spent running around on the farm flooded me. But here I was, on my first day at my new school.

Taking my place at lunch among my new friends, I was approached by a kind lunch lady. Her gentle eyes sparkled as she handed me a plastic cup of milk. The creamy whiteness of the liquid seemed to glow in the sunlight, inviting me into a moment of pure indulgence. I raised the plastic cup to my lips, savoring the velvety texture. Each sip was a revelation, the sweet creaminess a luxurious experience.

With every new friendship forged and every indulgent sip

of milk savored, the once-familiar walls of my world—which was only the farm and my grandparents' home—began to expand. I was swept up in a vivid whirlwind of flavors, companionship, and the exhilarating promise of knowledge.

My years at school progressed without much to derail me, and my grandfather was a pillar of support. He would share pearls of wisdom that lit the way through my academic challenges. His encouragement nurtured my curiosity and thirst for knowledge, guiding me through countless discoveries until I reached the transformative stage of completing high school.

In the excitement of learning and the thrill of new ideas, my thoughts often drifted toward my biological mother. I began to have very faint memories of her laughter. Were these my real memories? Or was it my mind making it up so I would have some connection to her? Each day at school, as I delved into history, science, and social studies, unanswered questions clawed at me with increasing urgency.

One day in sixth grade, I sat at my desk, surrounded by the lively chatter of my peers in the classroom and the scratching of pencils on paper. The teacher's voice drifted in and out of my focus as my mind wandered, wrestling with the profound family mysteries that had haunted me for years. Outside, the sun streamed through the windows, casting checkered patterns on the floor, each square a reminder of the fragmented memories of my mother. I had kept all my questions locked away in the depths of my heart—questions that had gone unanswered for far too long. As I stared at the neatly arranged rows of textbooks, the words blurred, giving way to images of a woman I barely knew. My mind wandered so far from the classroom, I felt I was on a different plane of consciousness altogether.

The stark facts of my reality prevented me from reaching out and bridging the gap between my mother and me. I longed for clarity, for a connection that had been denied to me. I felt trapped in this void, silent and vast. No one could see me or hear me, nor could I see them or hear them. Fear and uncertainty held me captive in this expanse that seemed to reach into infinity.

Suddenly, the school bell rang. Its sharp clang jolted me from my strange and vivid daydream and back to the chair I sat in, pencil in hand, paper in front of me on the desk. My classmates began to file out of the room, their laughter echoing in the school courtyard. I felt glued to my chair, unable to move. It took all of my strength to gather my books, my heart so heavy, the weight of my situation pressing down on me. Though the school day had ended, the maze of my emotions followed me home.

CHAPTER FOUR

My thirst for understanding my mother was growing, yet I was trapped, unsure how to articulate my emotions or which trusted confidant to turn to. The yearning for connection with my mother only deepened as I lived through the challenges of adolescence, silently seeking answers to profound questions about my identity and her place in my life. My daydreams continued. I envisioned our long-awaited reunion, promising myself that once we were together, I would never let her go again.

Gradually, my uncles regaled me with stories of when I was a toddler and my mother's visits during those years. Of course, I was too young to have any real memory of those visits. But my uncles painted vivid scenes of her spirited escapades. One particular day remains etched in Uncle Patrick's memory as he reminisced about my childhood. I sat beside him, my heart pounding, eager to hear the story of my mother unfold.

Uncle Patrick's gaze drifted into the distant layers of time, drawing forth memories from a place that perhaps began long before I was born, his voice full of nostalgia and sorrow. He spoke as though she were my mother and Greg were my father; however, Patrick and the rest of my family never recognized the emotional turmoil that these names and terms were causing me. It was as if, when they spoke of my true mother and my true father, the words were interchangeable, carrying no weight at all. It was as if up was down, and down was up, and this switch didn't make a bit of difference to them.

"When I think back to your childhood," Uncle Patrick said, "your mother..." His words made me freeze. He knew that I knew, but he wasn't going to acknowledge it directly. "She was a vibrant force of nature, bursting into the house like a ray of sunshine breaking through dense fog. The air itself shimmered with her presence. One day, you were playing inside." The corners of his mouth lifted in a soft smile. "In a moment of spontaneity, she scooped you up into her arms, cradling you against her, and whisked you away on an adventure, blissfully unaware of the anxious eyes of family watching from a distance. An unspoken tension lurked. We could all feel it."

"Hours drifted by like the gentle passage of clouds. But soon, the unsettling realization of your absence began to creep into our minds. A woman, out for her leisurely afternoon stroll, caught sight of your mother leading you down the street. With a furrowed brow, she observed a troubling sight—your mother's movements appeared erratic, her steps unsteady, as if the very ground she stood on was shifting. The woman approached us. 'I'm worried,' she said. 'I saw her struggling to carry the boy.' Apparently you had tumbled from your mother's back several times."

I listened intently to my uncle, emotions stirring within me. There was an insatiable curiosity about my mother's experiences, sympathy for her struggles, and yearning to understand the woman whose spirit shaped my life.

"When your father returned home, he was met with an unsettling silence that loomed over our usually lively place," my uncle continued. "Fear coiled in his stomach as he sensed something was amiss. Panic surged through his veins as he leaped onto his bicycle. The wheels spun rapidly against the dusty road as he raced toward the nearby village of Abuko. This was not an isolated incident. All of her visits were full of concerning events like this. All of them."

Patrick recounted that whenever my father picked me up from my mother's place, he sometimes found me alone, without any adult supervision. When my mother finally returned, her gaze was distant, and a heavy haze clouded her bloodshot eyes, as if she had temporarily retreated to a familiar yet foggy realm of her own mind. It was clear that her thoughts were consumed by something far removed from the present.

When my father confronted her about why she had left me

alone and where she had disappeared to, tense arguments erupted between them. Loud voices clashed in the once-peaceful yard. Each disagreement seemed to peel back layers of buried frustration and unresolved issues.

"Did she ever tell Greg where she had been or why she had left me alone?" I asked Patrick, seeking a better explanation.

He shrugged, his expression betraying a mix of concern and helplessness.

On those afternoons when my mother would abruptly take me out, only to abandon me shortly afterward, I wondered if she was attempting to mend something broken in our relationship. Was she lost in her own struggles, desperately seeking to connect while simultaneously trying to escape from emotions? I couldn't yet comprehend. What traumas or hardships had she endured in her youth that shaped such turbulent patterns in her behavior? More questions weighed heavily on my mind.

But then Uncle Patrick smiled at me; his expression was now warm and understanding. "Though this story may be difficult to hear, it's vital to remember that your mother loved you deeply, with a fierce devotion, and our family came together during times of hardship. Never underestimate the transformative power of love and resilience; they are the enduring bonds that connect us and guide us through life's trials, illuminating our path forward."

At that moment, Patrick did begin to acknowledge how I

had been feeling. It made me feel better. These stories from my uncle were not moments of distress for me; they infused me with bits of comfort. They helped me stitch together threads of our family history. Listening to those tales also ignited a deeper sense of yearning for memories I never had the chance to create in real time. I was too young to recall the warmth of my mother's embrace, the melodic sound of her laughter, or the delightful mischief we could have shared. All those stories became my lifeline to those lost moments, bridging the gaps my own memory couldn't fill and allowing me to connect with my past.

I moved forward with the hope that, in time, the elusive image of my mother would continue to become clearer, emerging from the mists of memory like a beacon guiding me home.

I have one memory that I know was mine and mine alone; it was not based on what Patrick told me. I know that this day happened when I was very young, and I recalled it as I reflected more on my childhood.

A beautiful woman of fair complexion came to my grandparents' home. She stood in the doorframe as if she were a figure stepping out of a scene from a fairy tale. She looked poised and elegant. Upon entering our home, she greeted my grandparents with warm affection, wrapping them in a fond embrace.

When she turned her attention toward me, her voice

chimed out, "John!" It was a calling that resonated within me, yet my feet felt rooted, and my eyes remained locked onto her with a mixture of awe and doubt. As I stood there, my heart raced, fueled by a swirl of emotions I couldn't quite put my finger on. My grandparents, sensing my hesitation, urged me to approach her. "That is…your mother. Go say hello."

Standing there, I felt conflicting emotions—anger, sadness, confusion. A heavy uncertainty gripped me, slowing my movements and heightening my anxiety as I cautiously made my way toward her. The woman's words seemed to drift in and out of my consciousness. I still could not fully grasp who this woman really was.

Moments later, the sound of my grandfather's voice broke through my internal turmoil. His tone was tinged with frustration and concern as he addressed my mother. "Why haven't you come to visit your child? He is your son, and no one is stopping you from entering this house. You are always welcome here."

Thinking back, I can recall the woman's eyes were bloodshot and clouded. The scent of something sour wafted off her and lingered in the air. As I watched her leave the house, unexpected relief washed over me. I was free from the burden of emotions that had been unearthed. These were emotions I seemed to prefer to keep buried all these years. But I had met her. And perhaps I was finally old enough to process it.

CHAPTER FIVE

In my mother's absence, I continued to seek comfort in the nurturing presence of my grandparents, uncles, and cousin Kujungs. Following the dissolution of her parents' marriage, Kujungs came to live with us, quickly becoming a radiant beacon of light in my murky world. She filled a void in my heart, a cherished friend who embodied the innocent spirit of a little sister.

Kujungs was a couple of years younger than I was, and after she moved in, we ended up attending the same school. Life settled into a routine that felt as normal as possible under the circumstances. Together, Kujungs and I would help our grandmother prepare meals in the kitchen. We also tackled our chores on the farm, working alongside our grandparents in the fields, and spent countless afternoons playing together at home, building forts with blankets or exploring the woods nearby.

Kujungs remained blissfully unaware of my biological

parents' identities. I think she simply accepted the story everyone had crafted—that my grandparents were my real parents. It was a narrative that had been repeatedly reinforced, and it provided a sense of stability for everyone.

Kujungs had her own set of concerns with her family. She only saw her mother on weekends, a situation that must have been challenging for her. Despite that, they shared a strong mother-daughter bond, which might have made it even harder for Kujungs to be separated from her.

As the years passed and we matured, I sensed that Kujungs began to piece together the complexities of my situation on her own. In keeping with the unspoken rules of our family, no one broached the subject directly. Despite the closeness I felt with my cousin, considering her a confidante and sibling, I found it impossible to discuss my own struggles with her. I remained silent, holding back the truth that weighed heavily on my heart, at least for the time being. This reticence was characteristic of our upbringing, a reflection of the culture and norms where we lived, especially during our formative years, when emotional vulnerability was rarely expressed.

During my teenage years, I stumbled a bit while my curiosity bubbled beneath the surface. My mind often raced with questions that I never voiced aloud: What is really going on with my mother? Why does it feel as though she doesn't care about me at all? Fear kept these questions locked away inside me. The thought of confronting my grandparents was daunting.

Then worry began to gnaw at me relentlessly. What if I never find my mother? If I had some way to call her or track her down, then—but soon the feeling of being lost returned. I was unsure of how I could possibly locate my mother by myself. With each passing year, my resolve to connect with her—despite her apparent disinterest in my life—only deepened.

Beyond my longing to find my mother, and with no access to technological devices that might have helped, poverty itself was a constant and distressing weight. Ensuring our safety from both external threats and internal strife took precedence. This constant state of vulnerability made us particularly susceptible to the superstitions and myths that often flourish in the darkness of hardship.

I couldn't shake the feeling that our financial struggles allowed others to dismiss us, attributing our misfortunes to some malevolent force rather than acknowledging the harsh and unforgiving realities we endured. Every morning, I would wake up to the familiar sight of our mud house, its ragged thatched roof sagging under the weight of time and harsh weather. Even after my grandfather devoted every ounce of his energy to patching the beleaguered roof, and as his financial situation improved, these small victories provided only momentary relief, just droplets in the vast ocean of adversity that threatened to engulf us.

Kujungs and I still used those plastic bags as makeshift backpacks for school, but saw that it was a common practice among many children in similar circumstances. When we returned home from school, our grandparents insisted we remove our shoes, as they were our only pair.

The soft glow of candlelight danced across our faces as we gathered around the time-worn wooden table. Christmas Day was approaching, and the excitement was palpable, brimming with the promise of a meal that would transport us, even if just for a fleeting moment, into a realm of comfort and abundance. My grandmother, her cheeks aglow from the flickering warmth of the three-stone fire, stepped away from the kitchen, her hands cradling a steaming pot of rich stew. The enticing scent made our home cozy and inviting.

"Ooh, she cooked tender beef!" I exclaimed, my mouth watering in anticipation. "This and the perfectly fried rice will taste fantastic!"

As Nteh ladled the stew onto a large communal plate, we gathered around the table, eager to share and savor the delicious feast. Dressed in our new shoes and carefully chosen clothes, we felt a sense of pride and joy, each piece a testament to my grandparents' love and sacrifices. These items of clothing were not merely material possessions; they symbolized the magic that could illuminate even the darkest of times. Together, we clasped our hands in prayer, a moment of reverent silence, offering gratitude, unity, and a much-needed break from the challenges we faced each day. Laughter erupted around the table, and we shared stories.

On that one festive evening, the usual burdens that tethered us to the ground were momentarily cast aside. In their place was the warm embrace of family, the satisfying fullness of a hearty meal that lingered in our bellies, and the profound realization that, despite our hardships, we were rich in the most essential treasures: love, hope, and the resilience to forge ahead.

As the last light of that festive day faded, Kujungs and I ran out the front door, stepping into the crisp night air. Our friends beckoned us to join in a timeless game of hide and seek. "We can't wait to play!" we would exclaim, our voices echoing in the darkness of the night. We dashed around the yard, weaving between trees and ducking behind fences, each giggling and shouting until our energy began to wane. Eventually, we found ourselves panting as the fatigue of play set in, and it was time to go to bed. "Ah, what a beautiful night," I said. These were the cherished memories that remain etched in my heart forever—not merely for me, but for countless others who were able to savor similar delights, finding joy in the simple, yet profound moments of friendship and life.

My young adult life, though, seemed to stretch across a more treacherous landscape. I realized that the specter of poverty was not our sole affliction. When I was in my teens, Baba married a second wife, Lena. In The Gambia, polygamy was common and legally recognized, so this second marriage of

Baba's was generally okay, and he did seek my grandmother's approval to do this. Baba and Lena had another baby, Mado, named after Baba's first wife, my grandmother, whose given name was also Mado. Greg, Patrick, and Jose had a half-sister, and I now had a step-grandmother and a half-aunt. Even if baby Mado was a decade and a half younger than I was, I still cherished this new relationship.

But despite the extending branches of our family tree, we faced dark rumors of witchcraft and sorcery. These insidious rumors soiled our reputation within the community and held an unsettling power over our neighbors, compelling many to distance themselves from us, consumed by fear and superstition.

I vividly recall one chilly evening, I was playing with the neighborhood children. As darkness settled in, their mother called them home, her voice a stern reminder of the time. The following day, one of the kids approached me with a pained expression and said, "Our mother doesn't want us to play with you because she believes you are the child of witchcraft parents."

Those words pierced my heart, leaving me feeling hurt and isolated. Despite the malicious gossip, my family found refuge among those who either chose to dismiss the rumors or remained blissfully oblivious to the malignant tales swirling around us. My grandparents, who were both strong and weary, bravely bore the brunt of the unfounded accusations. They endured slurs such as "the devil's disciples," "witches," and "wizards"—labels that clung to them with a stubbornness akin to weeds refusing to be uprooted. While some neighbors turned their backs on my grandparents, others continued to visit, showing a willingness to offer support and friendship.

The damaging stigma of witchcraft also reached my father, ensnaring him in a web of suspicion that painted him as a menacing figure, accused of preying upon the vulnerable to sustain the alleged sorcery of my grandparents. One afternoon, my father approached a neighbor's compound and caught snippets of conversation from a small group of people standing just behind a fence, whispering.

"They say he is the one! Greg is the one who is feeding his parents' dark power."

As my father stepped into the compound, their voices fell silent, the atmosphere tensing as they abruptly changed the subject and exchanged forced greetings, leaving my father to bear the heavy burden of their disdain in silence. Whispers of witchcraft and dark magic loomed over our entire family.

Even I was not immune to suspicion; some of my childhood friends called me a witch. Each day I had the heavy burden of rejection, loneliness, and despair. With poverty conditions and my missing mother, now my friends were turning against me for no just cause. What once was a source of happiness—playing football and other games—became uncomfortable as escalating rumors drove a wedge between me and my friends. They constantly taunted me, claiming that I was "too strong" because of the supposed "human meat" I consumed and the "wings" I used to fly at night.

The vibrant, dusty soccer field stretched out before me, a vivid canvas of faded green marked by deep trenches where countless cleats had dug into the earth. Its inviting expanse, however, was now tainted by the cruel whispers that twisted around me. As I positioned myself at the edge of the field at the start of a training session, the familiar weight of the ball resting against my foot felt more like an oppressive burden than a source of joy and freedom. The thrill of the game, once a pure delight, had become overshadowed by a sense of dread.

"Hey, witch boy!" taunted a former friend, his voice dripping with malice as it sliced through the crisp evening air. "Don't use your powers to win the game, alright?"

I fought to ignore his jibe, focusing instead on the rhythmic rise and fall of my breath and the gritty texture of the soil beneath my feet, anxiously seeking solace in those familiar sensations. When the trainer blew the whistle and the game commenced, a rush of adrenaline surged through me. For a brief moment, I was lost in the exhilarating dance of players darting across the field, caught up in the thrill of pursuing the ball and winning the competition. Each time I scored a goal, a euphoric surge of triumph filled me, but fresh jeers from the sidelines swiftly brought back that nagging feeling.

"Must be those wings, eh?" they mocked, tearing at the once-strong bonds of camaraderie that had connected us. Those bonds, now frayed and fragile, reminded me of the painful reality I faced.

As the sun dipped below the horizon, painting the sky in hues of deep orange and purple, the field fell into an unsettling twilight. I stood apart from my teammates, my isolation becoming a physical manifestation of the rumors. Their betrayal throbbed within me. Yet, I realized my journey had morphed into one of resilience and inner strength. I resolved to carry the burden of my innocence, determined to rise above the prejudice and fear that threatened to define me. I sought comfort in the knowledge that, one day, the truth would emerge eventually, and I would feel free once again.

I tried to understand the perplexing question of why my grandparents, my father, and I were labeled as witches and wizards. In many regions of Africa, the belief in witchcraft remained entrenched, intricately woven into the culture of communities. This pervasive belief often led to tragic consequences, as lives were shattered in an instant when accusations arose. The mention of witchcraft accompanied a whirlwind of social stigma, prompting severe mental anguish and ostracism from friends, neighbors, and even family members. Allegations surfaced in the wake of a tragic death, marking an innocent family member a target for blame. Similarly, those who faced debilitating illnesses, elderly individuals without the protection of adult children, widows left to live in the world alone, or people engulfed by extreme poverty often found themselves ensnared in these frightening labels. Additionally, individuals dealing with mental health challenges were marked in this way, condemned by a society that didn't want to understand their plight.

The labeling of our family as witches and wizards was not just a haunting stigma; it became a painful reminder of how swiftly compassion was overshadowed by fear and ignorance. It illustrated the desperate human tendency to find someone to blame in a world that frequently felt chaotic and unkind.

Although this rejection from friends, neighbors, and others in our community was incredibly painful, I wanted to feel connected to a larger group somehow. I had to counterbalance this rejection with an acceptance somewhere and to fill a need in my social life. While in high school, I decided to join the church choir, the Holy Rosary Choir, which unexpectedly became a pivotal experience for me. It was in this harmonious setting that I developed a strong relationship with a group of people I had known casually for some time but had never considered true friends until this point. I eventually found solace, support, and loyalty from individuals who stood by my side during that difficult time, and I continue to cherish those deep bonds to this day.

Attending choir practice at least twice a week allowed us to share our love for music and fostered a sense of camaraderie that drew us closer together. I suspected that some of them may have heard the rumors surrounding my situation, but they either chose not to discuss it with me or simply remained unaware of the details. Regardless, the friendships I formed during the choir were invaluable.

We started hanging out almost every day, creating unforgettable memories and supporting each other through life's highs and lows. Some of the main members of our group included Mbahal, with his contagious laughter; Simoni, who always shared insightful thoughts; Badou and Beni, who loved discussing music; Dave, known for his steady loyalty; and Apache, whose kindness made him a favorite among us all. Together, we formed a close-knit community that enriched my life in ways I never expected.

During our choir practice, the room buzzed with lively energy as we gathered, our voices harmonizing. Amid the occasional out-of-tune note, there was playful teasing. "Why do you sound like a goat?" someone would call out, prompting laughter. Another might chime in with a cheeky grin, "You look like you're about to cry when we reach that high note!" This friendly ribbing created a comfortable, familiar atmosphere, transforming what could have been a stressful rehearsal into a delightful gathering of friends. Each session fostered a sense of belonging, ensuring we weren't just individuals coming together to sing, but a close-knit family united by our passion for music and our appreciation for each other's unique quirks. As the laughter subsided and the music began anew, we embraced both the challenges and triumphs, knowing that these moments were the threads weaving us together in a beautiful tapestry of friendship.

CHAPTER SIX

Throughout this time, when I faced a tarnished reputation and rejections, my beloved grandfather, whose wisdom ran deep, emerged as the bedrock upon which my character and resilience were forged. On frigid nights, he would gather us close around a crackling fire, the flames dancing and casting flickering shadows against the darkness. His words served as a beacon of strength.

With a gentle but firm voice, he urged me to remain steadfast in my resolve. "Place your faith in God," he said. "There are brighter days coming to soon break through your dark clouds."

Kujungs and I would snuggle closer to him. These fireside conversations and moments of familial unity were more than mere comfort to us. They became profound lessons in perseverance and hope, a cherished experience I fondly referred to as "School with Baba."

Even with the connection to my choir friends and the

support from Kujungs, Nteh, and Baba, the darkness would seep back every once in a while. Conflicting emotions swirled within me, and the unanswered questions about my mother bothered me.

I stood at the window of my room, gazing upon the darkening sky, where ominous clouds roiled and clashed, mirroring the storm that churned in my heart. I envisioned my mother, her face etched with lines of worry. Where was she? How was she doing? Was she okay? Did she ever think about me?

Overwhelmed by despair, I sank to my knees, tears cascading down my cheeks—a testament to the fears that consumed my every thought. My hands clenched into tight fists, grasping the worn fabric of my trousers, seeking an anchor amid all the unknowns. Each labored breath felt as though it drew in the entire world, my chest heaving with anxiety.

The first raindrops pattered against the windowpane, and I felt the heaviness of my burden settle upon me. The suffocating weight of my mother's plight intertwined with the daunting uncertainty of my future. Yet, even as the encroaching darkness threatened to consume me whole, a small spark flickered deep within—a stubborn ember of hope that refused to be extinguished. With a trembling hand, I reached for the tattered journal resting beside me. I grabbed a pencil and began to write.

I had filled pages and pages with my dreams, goals, and

fragile promises. Writing in my journal had sustained me through countless sleepless nights, and it would again on this night. I often found solace in writing, weaving my aspirations into words that reflected my deepest desires. I would write, "When I grow up, I want to make a profound and lasting impact on society by helping those who are vulnerable and in need, much like the challenges I have faced throughout my life." I envisioned my role as a beacon of hope, striving to "positively influence people's perspectives and beliefs," bringing warmth and understanding to hearts that may feel weary and weighed down by the world. In addition to this calling, I harbored a burning passion for soccer, dreaming of one day standing on the hallowed grounds of Old Trafford, proudly wearing the iconic red jersey of Manchester United. I could picture myself dazzling fans with skillful plays while representing my country with pride on the grand international stage.

Alternatively, my imagination took me to the realm of architecture, where I dreamed of becoming one of the most revered architects in history, dreaming up structures that would not only inspire awe but also build connections within communities. These grand ambitions fueled my spirit and ignited a sense of purpose that propelled me forward each day.

Yet, amid these dreams lay that heavy ache in my heart, that deep longing for my mother, whose absence followed me all my life. The uncertainty of her whereabouts and the unknowns of her existence weighed heavily on my soul, often bringing tears to my eyes. I vowed with every fiber of my being that one day I would bridge the gap between us. I envisioned a future where we would reunite, cultivating a bond that was not only strong but filled with joy and celebration, ensuring that she would know happiness and experience the love we both so desperately yearned for.

My fingers traced the lines in my journal, each defiant word imbued with the potential of a future where my struggles would transform into a beacon of inspiration, guiding others through their own tumultuous journeys. With the storm roaring and raging outside, I clung fiercely to that fragile spark. My heart ached with the knowledge that the road ahead would be riddled with obstacles. But in the eye of the storm, I found the strength to confront the darkness that loomed before me, daring to dream of a brighter tomorrow—a day that would rise triumphantly from the deepest despair.

Every tick of the clock resonated in my mind, an ever-present reminder of the deafening silence between me and my mother. My heart ached with the haunting possibilities of the difficulties she could be confronting at that very moment—whether she was struggling against the unyielding forces of nature, battling unforeseen obstacles on her path, or enduring the profound longing for the warmth and solace of home. The same questions repeated in my mind. Where was she? Who was she with? What was happening to her? Was she safe, scared, lonely?

I was worried. I wanted answers. My every waking

moment was consumed with restless contemplation. Though hope flickered, I felt afraid and exhausted. I didn't quite know what to do.

CHAPTER SEVEN

In the autumn of 2000, a significant change occurred for our family when Uncle Jose embarked on a journey to the United States. His departure marked a crucial turning point in our circumstances. Once he found work, he began sending money home to us, which gradually improved our living conditions. Uncle Jose became my educational sponsor, providing the support I needed to complete my schooling and ultimately graduate from an architectural program. In addition to his financial contributions, he would send clothes and small gifts whenever possible, reminding us that we were loved and that love knows no boundaries.

Over time, the accusations of witchcraft that had isolated our family faded, and people in our community weren't as distant as they once were. Those who had kept their distance slowly re-emerged, though cautiously. I would get a smile or small greeting from someone while I was out in town, and at first I felt surprised, but then I decided to think nothing of it.

If the other people in our town decided that this malicious gossip was no longer hanging over my family or me, then I would as well.

With Uncle Jose's support, we were able to build a beautiful house on the same land that we had been living on since my childhood, and for the first time in years, we regularly enjoyed good, nourishing food on our table.

Also during this time, my father Greg remarried a woman named Yayo, but that marriage was short-lived; by 2008, they divorced amicably. I had a very good relationship with my stepmother despite the separation from my father.

Then, later in 2008, my father and Uncle Patrick followed in Uncle Jose's footsteps and made their way to the United States, further solidifying our family's newfound stability, albeit with a significant geographical separation. This turn of events was exciting for everyone in the family, even though we would miss my father and uncles so much.

Having relatives in the United States was a source of pride for family members, especially with those who lived in Western countries, most notably the United States. There was a sense that life would be better. They would help financially and elevate our status among our neighbors. Our status had taken a hit with the unfounded rumors of witchcraft, but now we had three family members living in the United States. Things were looking up.

Late one evening, I returned home from choir practice, the sounds of music still echoing in my mind. With my family all asleep, I walked quietly to my room so as not to wake anyone. An unusual sight greeted me. My bed was strewn with clothes, lotion, and a myriad of other items that seemed completely out of place. Confusion washed over me, then I realized it was Valentine's week. My imagination took flight, conjuring various scenarios. Maybe these were Valentine's gifts? I had recently begun a friendship with someone special, but there was no planned visit from this new friend at all during that week. So who came to my house to give me gifts? My curiosity piqued, and I resolved to ask my family the following day, hopeful that they could unravel the mystery.

In the morning, my chest fluttered with anticipation. I went into the kitchen to see my grandfather, stepmother Yayo, and Aunt Mado at the table with their cups of tea. I fully expected them to explain the gifts. As I stood before them, the air electric, I asked, "Who gave me these gifts?"

"It was your mother," Baba revealed softly, his words sending a jolt of surprise coursing through me. "She arrived late last night while you were at choir practice."

His revelation sank in slowly, and in that moment, a mix of emotions crashed over me—disbelief, joy, confusion, and a flicker of hope. My mother, the elusive figure who up to this point in my life had been a distant memory—a mere whisper from my past—had come to visit. She had shown up at my house to give me carefully chosen gifts as a testament to her love and presence.

The assortment of items now radiated with significance. Though my mother's presence was fleeting, the profound meaning of her late-night visit and the gifts resonated within me, a bittersweet reminder of the unbreakable bond between a mother and her child—a bond that can withstand the passage of time and the barriers of distance.

I scanned the room, hoping she would be there. My heart quickened with excitement at the thought of seeing my mother for the first time since I was young, yearning for the opportunity to finally connect with her and have a heartfelt conversation after so long. "Is she awake? Let's go wake her now."

"She didn't stay the night," my grandfather said. "She dropped off the gifts, then left."

"Why?" I asked. "Why would she only stay a minute and not even wait until I came home? Didn't you tell her that I would be back right after choir?"

"I must confess to you that as soon as she arrived, I told her she needed to stop drinking. I don't think she wanted to hear that from me. She left not long after I said that." My grandfather then told me he believed that if she stopped drinking, she could foster a long-overdue connection between us. "Unfortunately," he continued, "she chose to spend the night at our neighbor's house."

Anger and sorrow rushed through me, emotions I was well-acquainted. The familiar sting of disappointment surged within me, prompting me to seek better answers from my grandfather. Her decision to leave and go to the neighbors felt like a betrayal.

I looked at Baba, my eyes searching his eyes for understanding, desperately seeking an explanation for my mother's cycle of intoxication. What could possibly be the cause of her drinking habits?

"My son, I am so sorry that you have to deal with this issue regarding your mother."

A sense of urgency gripped me; I needed to confront the situation head-on. Without wasting a moment, I marched toward the neighbor's house, driven by determination and anxiety.

As I neared the house, I saw her. This was the first time as a young adult that I would come face-to-face with my mother. My chest was pounding.

She sat outside on the neighbor's porch, cradling a cup filled with what I could only guess was alcohol. The sight of her, so vulnerable and lost, beautiful and fragile, caused my heart to sink. I could see myself in her—her eyes like mine, my hair like hers—it was obvious we were related.

Approaching her cautiously, I softened my voice, striving to mask the turmoil swirling within me. "Let's go back to Baba's house."

"He's trying to control me. He wants to take charge of my life," my mother said.

"Who? Baba?"

"Yes."

That response was a dagger to my heart. Refusing to budge, my mother stated she wouldn't return with me. I was so disappointed, but I refused to give in to despair. "Please come back with me. I've waited years to see you and have a real conversation with you. My whole life, I have wanted this." I poured my heart into each word until, at last, she agreed to come back with me.

As we made our way home, I could see the understanding in my grandfather's eyes—it was clear he knew just how intoxicated she was. In a silent plea for discretion, I gestured for him to remain quiet. My heart swelled with gratitude when he honored my request.

Although my mother was physically present beside me, I knew her mind was lost in a fog, and any hope for a meaningful conversation drifted further away like smoke in the wind.

"I want to visit a relative of mine who's just a couple of blocks away from here," my mother eventually said.

Knowing we couldn't make her stay, no matter what we said or how hard we pleaded, we decided to just let her go, hoping this would provide her with the comfort she was seeking.

CHAPTER EIGHT

The day I saw my mother on the neighbor's porch marked another turning point in my life, reshaping my perspective on our complicated relationship and igniting a determination within me to confront it. With feelings of frustration and disappointment, I grappled with a sense of powerlessness. Nonetheless, I held on to the hope that one day my mother and I would bridge the gap that had developed between us, allowing us both to heal the deep-seated wounds from our past.

As we began to spend more time together, I noticed specific behaviors that were troubling; it was clear to me that something was not right with her. My mother's actions often seemed erratic. Yet, in certain moments, I was trapped in denial, refusing to fully acknowledge the extent of her struggles. I felt isolated in my thoughts, unable to share with anyone else. But I remained strong in my conviction that I should never give up on her. I believed I was uniquely positioned to make a difference, as if I were the only person in her life, in this world, capable of helping her find her way back to a healthier state.

I struggled with the complexities of our relationship, yearning for connection while also feeling pain and bitterness. Several days after my mother dropped gifts off for me, I received an unexpected phone call from a colleague. He spoke with amusement and concern, informing me that there was some sort of commotion somewhere around our house, as was often the case.

"It could be your mother."

"How do you know?" I asked.

Before he could answer, a sinking feeling settled in my stomach. I immediately suspected it was my mother. "Just tell me where, and I'll go see for myself," I added.

My heart raced as I dashed toward the site he mentioned, anxiety pushing me forward. Upon my arrival, I was met with a disheartening sight. A group of people had gathered, as if a party had just started right there in the street. There was a woman in the center. It was my mother—I was sure of it. I recognized many of the townspeople who were gathered around her; I had spent time with their children. They were all giggling.

I couldn't stand by and watch my mother's strange behavior in front of everyone. In a fit of anger, I grabbed her arm and pulled her away from the crowd, raising my voice as

I demanded, "Mother, what are you doing here?"

"Son, I am just dancing, and everyone here is dancing too. It is all just so much fun," she said with her eyes closed, swaying to music only she could hear.

"Is she really your mother?" someone asked me. I turned to see a man whose wrinkled brow showed he understood the palpable tension between my mother and me.

A heavy wave of shame hit me, pinching my heart. "Yes."

Shock rippled through the rest of the crowd. Everyone's mouths hung open.

One man hesitantly said, "We all assumed Nteh was your mother."

Everyone's surprise shifted to embarrassment. Soon they offered apologies, their voices laced with genuine regret. I saw their concerned glances.

I turned to my mother, my heart pounding with hope and desperation, "Please come home."

"No," she flatly refused. "I chose to remain at my relative's house."

I hurried home, urgency propelling me forward, eager to unburden my soul and share the shocking experience with my grandfather.

"People saw us, people heard me. Now everyone knows." I laid out the details of the unsettling encounter, and Baba's face, usually so strong and reassuring, cracked a bit. A visible vulnerability flickered in his eyes, a stark contrast to his typical stoicism. He felt my pain as if it were his own.

Baba placed his hand gently on my shoulder, the warmth of his touch a comforting contrast to the turmoil in my heart. With a soft yet firm voice, he said, "Do not to let this incident trouble you too much."

I could see the turmoil in his expression. In that moment, I realized we would get through this together.

Despite his comforting words and presence, I felt the heaviness of my emotions. I could no longer hold back the tears that had been threatening to spill; I ran to my room and sobbed for hours, the raw pain of feeling lost and betrayed flooding out of me.

Within the hour, my grandfather, stepmother, and Aunt Mado joined me in my solitude. Each of them offered their support in their own way, but it was Mado who truly connected with my grief. She sat beside me and cried alongside me, sharing in the depths of my sorrow, and her compassionate tears lent me a sense of solace.

The following day, my mother unexpectedly walked into our compound. Her demeanor was carefree, a stark contrast to the tumult of emotions I had carried since the previous day.

"I am here to take those gifts back," she said, heading straight to my room to collect them.

A desperate urge overcame me. "Please don't take those!" These material objects were my connection to her; though just bottles and fabric, their significance was so much deeper to me than just things on a shelf or hung in a closet.

Nonetheless, she gathered up the lotions and shirts. "I am going back to my relative's house." With her arms full of the items that were suddenly not mine anymore, she left.

Hours stretched into days, and I couldn't shake off the restlessness that gnawed at me. I resolved to take action and walked to the house of my mother's relative, where she was staying.

Each step felt heavier than the last, my mind racing with worry about her whereabouts and safety. Upon my arrival, I spotted a woman I recognized from family gatherings.

"Where is my mother?"

She looked at me with sympathy and concern, her eyes downcast as she said, "Sorry, son, but your mother has left and didn't tell us where she was going."

My heart plummeted. I shook my head, struggling to process the gravity of her words. I turned away, a crushing blend of hopelessness and defeat already settling in my chest.

As I made my way back home, a familiar sense of comfort pulled me toward my grandfather.

I found him sitting in his favorite armchair, and I took a deep breath. "She's left again. She's not even at their house."

He motioned for me to sit, his expression turning serious. "You need to have patience. And you know you're already so wise. Your thoughts are probably racing. Your emotions are everywhere. You know this house is a safe space to breathe and express yourself."

Gradually, I felt my anxiety begin to dissipate, thanks to his nurturing presence.

A few days later, my phone rang, and I noticed an unfamiliar number on the screen. My heart raced as I picked up, hoping it was my mother calling from her new location.

"Son," she said, her tone casual and almost nonchalant.

A lightness floated through my body. She sounded content and okay. However, that feeling didn't last long. The more she spoke to me, the more it became painfully clear that she was unaware of the turmoil her actions had caused in my life, especially in these past few days, as if those moments together had been insignificant.

I tried to probe her for more information. "Where are you? Where are you calling from?"

She skillfully dodged my questions. "I promise I will call you back soon with details about where I am staying. But I can't tell you now." Then she hung up.

I clung to that promise, waiting eagerly for her to reach out again, but the anticipated call never came. I tried to return the call to the number, but despite multiple attempts, my calls were not going through. It seemed as though the line was either busy or disconnected, making it impossible for me to reach her.

As days progressed into weeks and eventually months, my

thoughts constantly circled back to my mother, yet I chose to keep my worries bottled up inside, as was my habit. During this difficult period, I noticed a shift in my health; I began to experience high blood pressure, and I was only in my early twenties. This was a troubling symptom of the relentless anxiety stemming from my mother's puzzling absence and behavior.

Despite the turmoil inside me, I made a conscious effort to maintain a cheerful façade, greeting friends and acquaintances with a smile and pretending that everything was perfectly fine. They continued to see me as a happy person, blissfully unaware of the emotional storm that raged below the surface, a storm I had learned to mask.

During this time, singing in the church choir helped me get through my struggles and gave me a profound sense of solace. Not only did it deepen my faith in God, but it also offered a much-needed outlet for my emotions during tumultuous times. The act of singing, surrounded by a community of supportive individuals, allowed me to express feelings I could hardly articulate in words.

I also dedicated time to other outlets, including learning to play the piano, where I discovered the joy of creating music. I also picked up a bit of guitar, which introduced a new layer of creativity to my musical exploration. In addition to my musical pursuits, engaging in soccer with my colleagues proved to be another essential distraction. The dynamic energy of the game and the laughter shared with teammates was a welcome escape from the turbulent thoughts that overwhelmed me.

Spending time with my choir and soccer friends became an integral part of my routine. Whether we were grabbing something to eat, going for walks to the riverside, or simply hanging out, these moments of connection helped me temporarily evade the complexities of my mind, allowing for brief intervals of peace amidst the chaos of my thoughts. As I immersed myself in these activities, I began to realize just how vital my coping mechanisms were in helping me continue on this arduous journey.

Then, one fateful day, a female friend I had known for some time approached me with unexpected news that would change everything.

CHAPTER NINE

"There is someone in a neighboring country who is looking for you. She says she's your sister," my friend said.

My initial reaction was one of disbelief; laughter escaped me as I asked, "Who told you I have a sister in a neighboring country?"

Intrigued yet skeptical, I listened as my friend explained that this sister had given her a small piece of fabric to bring to me as a gift. "I recently met a lady in Casamance, a province in Senegal, who was actively looking for someone named John." My friend then handed me a piece of cloth that was vibrant green with swirls of other colors.

The cloth lay on my palm.

"I am confident that it is you." My friend's conviction was clear and sincere.

I couldn't help but feel a rush of gratitude for her bringing this vital information to me.

With this new knowledge weighing on my mind, I

gathered my thoughts and ran home to recount the startling revelation to my grandfather and my father.

With my grandfather across the living room table from me, and my father in the United States on speakerphone, I said, "I think there is a sister from my mother's side who is looking for me."

Baba's face was disbelief and astonishment. There was silence on the other end of the phone. For a moment, I thought our long-distance call had been disconnected. "Father? Are you still there?"

"Yes, I am. And this news is not surprising, but yet it is. I do not know what to think. What do you make of all this, John?"

What did I make of it? I made a vow to myself right there: I would find and meet my sister. I was convinced this part of the story held an important layer of truth.

As the weeks passed, a sense of uncertainty overcame me, an insistent reminder of the unanswered questions swirling in my mind. I replayed the details of the conversation with my friend, feeling an urgent need to speak with my mother to uncover more about this elusive sister I never knew existed.

One day, as I was going about my morning routine in the house—drinking tea, brushing teeth, locating matching socks—my phone rang, displaying a number again that I did not recognize. My heart raced, and my brain knew instantly who was calling. Could this be the breakthrough I had been yearning for?

Taking a deep breath, I answered the call with barely contained anticipation. I asked my mother pointedly, "Mother, do I have a sister in Casamance?"

There was a pause on the other end, creating a heavy silence before she finally responded. "Who told you that?"

"Mother, it doesn't matter who told me. What matters is the truth. I need to know the truth from you, please."

Another long and tense pause. "Yes," she finally said, "you have a half-sister. However, I insist that you should not worry about it."

"But I want to find her and meet—"

My mother hung up, leaving me in stunned silence.

Despite her dismissive attitude, that single confirmation ignited a fire within me; a newfound determination surged through my veins, compelling me to start on the quest to seek out my long-lost sister.

Feeling the gravity of the situation, I went to Baba. "I would like to ask for permission from you before taking any further steps."

He listened and contemplated. After a moment, he nodded. "You have my blessing to go find this person."

My grandfather's acknowledgment deepened my resolve. With confidence, I decided to call my father and discuss the subject with him. "I want to travel to a foreign country in search of my sister."

"Yes, you should. I support this decision of yours, and I will send you money for your journey," he said.

While I could hear the concern etched in his voice, his sending some money was a tangible symbol of his belief in me. I was comforted by his support and his help to pay for the travel I would need to get to where my sister was.

The friend who had initially informed me about my sister's existence played another pivotal role. She provided me with my sister's husband's phone number. I clung to the hope that this contact would serve as my lifeline on this venture. However, I learned that this sister and her husband lived in a remote area with limited communication options, adding to the uncertainty about my mission. What if the phone number didn't even work? It felt daunting, yet I was excited.

With my father's money securely in my pocket, I anxiously dialed my sister's husband's number. As the phone rang and rang, my stomach knotted with a mixture of adrenaline and apprehension. To my surprise and great relief, someone picked up.

"Hello?" a male voice said.

"Hello, I am John," I blurted out. "I might be related to your wife. I might be her half-brother." I didn't want him to hang up on me, thinking that perhaps I was a stranger calling, trying to scam him.

I explained my intention to visit and meet her. Every word felt surreal; the nerves coursed through me, making it hard to believe this was really happening.

"Oh, yes, she has been eagerly waiting to hear from you!" the man exclaimed. "Hold on a moment; here she is."

"My brother, I have been longing to see you for so many years." Her questions raced at me quickly. "How can we arrange a meeting? How is our mother doing?"

"So, Maria is your biological mother?" I tried to grasp the family connections.

"Yes!"

"That means the world to me. Okay, then, I will visit you next week; we have so much to discuss. I have to hang up soon because my phone credit is running low. Please tell your husband I will call him a day before I depart." As I hung up, joy washed over me.

A week later, I called my brother-in-law. "Tomorrow morning, I will be on my way," I announced. He provided me with clear, albeit brief, directions to their village.

Finally, my departure day was upon me. The sun was just beginning to rise as I left for Casamance. I boarded a rickety old bus, the interior filled with the warm chatter of passengers and the unmistakable scent of local spices. The journey lasted close to eight hours, and as we traversed winding roads, I marveled at the beautiful scenery through my window. There were lush fields dotted with wildflowers and majestic forests in the distance under a cobalt sky.

With each passing mile, my excitement grew. I had packed my backpack with care, ensuring my personal clothes were neatly folded within, ready for the reunion. During the bus ride, my mind was a jumble of questions. Would I really meet my sister? What did she know about our mother? Did she have a relationship with her at all? When did she find out about me? Would she accept me into her life after all these years?

As I entered my sister's country, I quickly came to the realization that I needed to obtain a new SIM card to facilitate proper communication. I had to buy one from one of the vendors lined up on the street and put it in my phone. The sun began to set, casting a warm glow over the unfamiliar landscape. When I reached my last stop late in the evening, my heart was racing.

There was my apparent brother-in-law, Totalla, standing on the roadside. Meeting him for the first time felt surreal; I was about to take a huge step toward discovering my sister. As we exchanged greetings, Totalla grinned and said, "Your sister will not believe this!"

At that moment, I had a realization: I had no clear idea of what my sister looked like or the kind of person she was. As we made our way through the rural village, I felt as if I had entered another world—one rich with vibrant colors, the sound of roosters crowing, and the scents of earth and cooking wafting through the air. The village was alive with activity; children darted through the narrow paths, their laughter ringing like music, while villagers tended to their daily chores, some working in gardens of lush greenery, others weaving intricate baskets from palm fronds.

As we walked past humble compounds adorned with bright cloths hanging from thatched roofs, inquisitive villagers paused in their routines, their eyes curious. One asked, "Who is this you're with? A new friend?"

Totalla responded with a friendly smile, "Ah, you're wondering why my wife's brother is here. He is beautiful, like my wife Neneth," he joked. His eagerness to lead me to my sister was palpable, and I felt my heart race even more.

Then, in a moment of this continuing dreamlike state, I noticed a slender figure sprinting toward me through the crowd of their big family that had gathered for the occasion. Tears flowed freely down her cheeks. As she drew closer, my pulse quickened with recognition, and it hit me. Neneth—this was my sister.

With no thought for decorum, I dropped my bag and broke into a run, my legs carrying me forward by an uncontainable force. When we collided in a fierce embrace, we wept into each other's shoulders. It was unbelievable. In that moment of pure vulnerability, I felt overcome with gratitude for finally having the opportunity to meet my sister face-to-face. As we pulled away, the surrounding villagers seemed just as excited about our reunion, eager to witness this long-overdue family connection.

After the tears of joy subsided, Neneth took my hand and said, "Come, sit, we have so much to tell each other."

My brother-in-law picked up my bag and continued into

the house. "I'll be in here. Come get me if you need anything."

Neneth and I found a shaded spot under a sprawling mango tree. Its thick leaves rustled gently in the breeze as we settled down. My sister began to share her life's story. "We struggle in this village, no electricity, we work on the farm all the time just to put food on the table. My kids are unable to go to school." Her eyes sparkled with passion as she recounted her experiences. "I have a wonderful marriage. We're very happy together." But then a palpable shift occurred in her voice. "I am disappointed with the way our mother has chosen to live her life."

It was evident the challenges Neneth and I had faced wove an unbreakable bond between us from the beginning. My sister admitted, "I haven't heard from our mother in ages. We cannot even try to contact her now. Neither of us has a phone number for her, nor do we know where she is. We have nowhere to call."

Feeling her words, I gently replied, "We should be hopeful, my dear sister. I know this is incredibly difficult for both of us, but it is essential that we try to move forward and embrace life to its fullest."

Our eyes locked. An unspoken understanding passed between us, affirming that we were not alone in our feelings.

During my three-day stay in the village, we engaged in captivating conversations. Each step revealed welcoming neighbors, whose smiles and kind gestures made me feel like part of a close-knit community.

Curiosity tugged at me as I pondered the thread that connected our lives, leading me to ask my sister, "How did you come to know about me?"

"Well, as I grew up, my aunt used to tell me tales of a brother waiting for me in The Gambia. She spoke fondly of our family lineage, and I clung to the names in her stories—your grandfather's name, your name, and the village where you reside with your grandparents. One day, your friend Fatima arrived in our village, introducing herself as hailing from your village. I was intrigued." She leaned closer. "I asked her if she recognized your grandfather, describing him as I was told, along with your name. To my astonishment, she confirmed that she knew both you and your entire family. In that moment, I sensed an undeniable connection, believing wholeheartedly that you were my long-lost brother. This is why I chose to send you a delicate piece of fabric and included my husband's phone number. I hoped you would call."

After spending three precious days full of laughter and sharing memories, I reluctantly prepared to leave and return home to my grandfather. As I said goodbye, my heart burst with love from the reunion. The visit had brought immense gratitude and relief. My sister and I had each other. Our bond would be unshakeable and enduring, regardless of the distance between us and our mother's absence.

Neneth and I remained in close contact, yet days turned into weeks, and still, there was no sign or word from our mother. It was as if she had vanished into thin air, leaving her children with ongoing uncertainty. We found ourselves questioning her whereabouts, imagining her in distant lands—perhaps wandering the bustling streets of The Gambia, embracing the vibrant culture of Senegal, or seeking solitude in the environment of Guinea-Bissau. Each possibility sparked a mix of hope and worry, amplifying our need for answers.

CHAPTER TEN

In the summer of 2014, I found myself standing before a life-changing opportunity—to study and stay in the United States, with the help of my father Greg and Uncle Jose. It was bittersweet.

Leaving my cherished friends, my dear grandfather, and my beloved siblings felt like tearing pieces out of my heart. Each goodbye was heavy with memories of laughter and love that I would miss. Adding to the emotional complexity was the thought of embarking on this new adventure without my mother's blessing and with continued uncertainty about her situation. Her absence affected me; I still grappled with the painful reality of not knowing her whereabouts and the unsettling notion that I would be traveling into the unknown without her even being aware of it.

In many African cultures, seeing children succeed and migrate to Western countries is a cherished dream for parents. It symbolizes hope for a brighter future, a beacon of pride in their hearts. As such, families often gather for a poignant farewell, surrounding their departing loved ones with prayers and blessings. For my sendoff, my family offered bittersweet goodbyes and wished me good luck on my journey into the unknown and the promise of a new adventure.

My flight to the United States originated in Senegal, so I would have to take a bus as the first leg of my voyage. On the day I was set to leave the familiar soil of The Gambia by bus, I packed a suitcase with old pairs of shoes and new clothes.

My grandfather stood before me with a warm, reassuring smile. He gave me his most sincere blessings and poured a libation to our ancestors for guidance. He said to me, "Go, John, and create a life for yourself that is full of love, wonder, and success. Never forget who you are and where you come from. This will influence your life."

Then I said farewell to my half-siblings. We all had tears.

When I stepped out of the compound that early morning, I felt a deep ache in my heart, especially when I glanced back to see my family still crying, their faces a mixture of sorrow and support.

As I made my way toward the bustling main road, where I would soon board the bus to Senegal, my grandfather's voice resonated with reminders of the unbreakable family bonds that would continue to connect us, no matter the distance.

"John," he had said, "if you hold on to all the advice I have shared with you, you will surely prosper in life. Always keep in mind that God comes first, and then, without a doubt, comes family. When you land there, remember to carry yourself as a visitor. A visitor is always cautious and maintains a certain reserve, for getting too comfortable can lead down a dangerous path, where bad choices and illegal activities may lurk." His words held wisdom and love, a reminder to stay grounded and true to the values we cherished.

I was about to leave for the United States, a land teeming with promise and opportunity. However, I felt I was leaving a part of myself behind in The Gambia.

I settled into the bus, and I couldn't help but notice Baba standing on the sidewalk, visibly emotional. His eyes shimmered with unshed tears, making it difficult for him to look directly at me. With a heavy heart, I waved goodbye, and he waved back, his hand trembling slightly. The bus began to pull away from my home. Profound sadness and worry swept over me. I felt I was abandoning him; after all, he had always been my confidant and friend. Our daily lunches, filled with laughter and shared stories, already began to feel like nostalgic memories.

Upon my arrival in Senegal, I had arranged to stay with relatives of my grandfather's. He had already informed them I was coming. When I found their house, I immediately called my grandfather to let him know I had arrived safely.

"I made it to Senegal!"

"I am so glad to hear from you, John, and I'm so proud and excited for you." Though his words were joyful, I could sense an undercurrent of sadness and loneliness, and that tugged at my heart.

The next morning, with only a single piece of luggage, I made my way to the airport in Dakar. A distant cousin, who was also staying at the family house, gave me a ride. Excitement bubbled inside me. I would be boarding an airplane for the first time.

My stomach fluttered as the force of the plane taking off pushed me farther into my seat. I looked out the window and saw the vibrant grounds of Africa getting smaller. I was leaving it all behind. I already missed Baba more than I could have ever imagined.

The trip was so extensive that it required multiple flights to reach my final destination in Denver, Colorado. At JFK International Airport, I navigated customs and immigration by myself. I vividly recall the warm and welcoming demeanor of the United States customs personnel, who made the process feel smooth and efficient. After successfully clearing that stage, I made my way to the departure gate, my hands sweating a bit with anticipation. The terminal buzzed with travelers from all walks of life, each with their own stories and destinations, making the airport feel like a community in itself. As I settled into my seat on the final flight, I couldn't help but imagine what awaited me in Denver.

As I stepped out of the jetway and into bustling DIA, the vibrant energy of the surrounding crowd added to my joy. I wandered through the frenetic airport, observing hurried travelers, the rich aroma of freshly brewed coffee from a nearby café, a family reuniting with ecstatic embraces, groups of young friends bursting into laughter. The colors of the airport's decorations—bold reds, cheerful yellows, and deep blues—contrasted beautifully against the sleek, modern architecture, enhancing the overall sense of liveliness. As I soaked in all the sights, smells, and sounds, my heart swelled with even more excitement. DIA was the exact opposite of our small and modest airport in The Gambia. I was in awe of the complete contrast.

My father and two uncles were waiting for me at baggage claim; they radiated with pride—their smiles wide enough to light up the entire terminal.

"Son, you made it!" Uncle Jose exclaimed, embracing me tightly.

My father smiled and added, "I'm so glad you made it here safely, my son."

Uncle Patrick stepped forward with a friendly grin, welcoming me to my new country. "But before we go any further," he said, quickly removing his thick jacket and draping it over my shoulders, "take this; it is chilly outside!"

The fabric was warm and comforting against my skin, making me feel immediately at home. I took my first steps on

American soil; I was finally living out a cherished dream.

I thought about the countless sacrifices my family had made to help me reach this point. I could hear their whispered hopes and aspirations propelling me into another thrilling chapter of my life. Every expectation rested on my shoulders, but it only fueled my determination to succeed and honor them.

We got to my father's home in Denver, where we gathered around the dining table to enjoy a hearty meal. We ate, shared stories, and reminisced. Then my father took me on a tour of the city, where he introduced me to the spouses and children of my two uncles. I met a cheerful group of cousins, each eager to share their own stories. My father also introduced me to a few of his friends, who welcomed me with smiles and banter.

We strolled through the downtown area, and I marveled at the impressive skyline that towered above us, composed of sleek glass buildings. The streets were alive with energy and friendly pedestrians. I couldn't contain my awe and excitement.

A few weeks later, I started my college journey at Aurora Community College. On the first day, I met a diverse group of international students. I felt very welcomed, and it made me feel as though I had found a little piece of home in an unfamiliar place. Each of the international students shared their own stories of culture shock and adjustment, and I could sense the camaraderie that comes from shared experiences. With their guidance, I figured out the process of signing up for classes and chose subjects like English, Math, and Human Psychology. It was reassuring to connect with others who understood the challenges of being new to the United States.

I quickly adapted to using the public bus system, which became my primary mode of transportation. I purposefully took different routes to the college each time so I could explore, hoping to find charming cafés and unique shops in my new city. Each day brought a new adventure.

Life was a bit challenging at first due to the Colorado altitude and the biting cold that sank into my skin in a way I had never experienced before. Not only did I have to deal with the colder climate, which required a wardrobe of layers I wasn't used to, but the altitude also affected my daily routine. Simple activities, like walking down a sidewalk, became daunting challenges as I ran the risk of slipping on ice or snow and of becoming winded or lightheaded.

Additionally, the cultural differences were striking. Everything from social norms to daily routines contrasted sharply with what I was used to. For instance, in The Gambia, greetings were characterized by lively handshakes and considerable physical contact, creating a sense of warmth and camaraderie that enveloped you in a comforting embrace. In Colorado, I discovered a more reserved approach to greeting one another, where hugs predominated but still felt a touch more distant.

Another key difference revolved around our relationship with time. In The Gambia, a relaxed, easy-going attitude permeated social life. Social engagements zipped along their own timetable, and it was perfectly acceptable for gatherings to start later than planned without raising an eyebrow. Conversely, in Colorado, I found that punctuality held significant weight; being on time was not just a courtesy but a mark of respect. The strict adherence to schedules often cast a strong sense of urgency over my experiences, leaving me feeling rushed and slightly anxious as I tried to keep pace with the fast-moving rhythm of life in Denver.

Moreover, the dynamics of social interactions showcased a striking divide between the two cultures. Gambian society thrived on the strength of extended families and deep community ties, where meeting new people was not only common but also easy and familiar, as if we were all woven into the same tapestry of human connection. However, in Colorado, I noticed a tendency among people to maintain a certain distance, especially with strangers. Many preferred solitude or engaged in reserved interactions, which made the process of forging new connections feel like an uphill battle. I longed for the effortless camaraderie that was a hallmark of my Gambian experience.

The local cuisine, while vibrant and full of flavors I had never encountered, was also a different from the dishes I grew up with. Each meal was an experience of its own, with unfamiliar ingredients and cooking styles. I can clearly recall the first time I encountered broccoli. My father chuckled softly as I gingerly poked at the green florets, my eyebrows knitted in confusion. I struggled to understand what I was looking at, declaring in frustration that I would never eat that peculiar vegetable again. Yet, as fate would have it, over the years, I grew to savor its earthy flavor and delightful crunch, becoming an enthusiastic fan of broccoli.

Sushi offered its own set of challenges. The first time I laid eyes on it, the neatly arranged rolls of raw fish and vinegared rice appeared foreign and intimidating. After my initial taste, which left me doubtful, I insisted I wouldn't touch it again. Years passed before I bravely revisited the culinary experience, and to my surprise, I was enchanted by the intricate flavors and textures; each bite weaving together hints of umami, freshness, and a touch of sea salt.

In those early days of trying new foods, every dish I ate felt as if it were drenched in an artificial sweetness, masking the natural flavors and nuances that lay beneath. But my palate eventually began to crave the rich blend of tastes that the culinary world offers, showing my journey from hesitant beginnings to a robust appreciation for diverse flavors.

I also noticed a remarkable contrast between grocery stores in the United States and the markets of The Gambia. One of the most striking differences was the meticulous organization and arrangement of products in American grocery stores. Each aisle boasted neatly stocked shelves, with items carefully categorized and labeled, creating an atmosphere of orderliness that simplified the shopping experience for customers. The grocery stores back home, referred to as markets, exuded an active and chaotic charm. The air was alive with sounds of vendors calling out to passersby, enticing them with shouts and deals on their fresh produce and handmade goods. Negotiating prices was not just common; it was an energetic dance of words, with both buyers and sellers engaging in spirited haggling.

As people walked through these bustling markets, they saw other vendors weaving through the throngs of shoppers, balancing baskets brimming with colorful fruits, fragrant spices, and vibrant vegetables. Many of them hoped to catch the eye of a potential buyer, often because they lacked the means to secure their own stall. The diverse colors, enticing aromas, and palpable sense of community in these markets created an unforgettable shopping experience that expressed the rich culture and spirit of The Gambia.

As the months went by, I attended classes, made friends, and grew accustomed to my new life in Denver. But then one day, after shopping at a nearby grocery store, I came home to see my father anxiously awaiting my return. The moment I walked in the door, brown paper bags still in my arms, he said to me, "Your cousin Dani called. You need to call him back. He saw your mother."

I called Dani immediately. He caught me up very quickly. Apparently, he had been out in the town of Farafenni, nestled on the northern side of The Gambia, and saw her.

"You spoke to her?"

"Yes, and she didn't know about you."

"What do you mean? Didn't know about me?"

"She didn't know you were in the United States now. She was completely unaware of your journey to America."

I could almost envision the moment—how her world shifted as her eyes widened with shock. Dani went on to describe how, upon hearing I had made it across the ocean, she was inundated with emotion. "John, she started to cry when I told her where you were," he said.

Dani assured me he would reach out again to both my mother and me, providing us the opportunity to reconnect for the first time in years.

The anticipation built within me as I waited one full day for his call. When Dani finally dialed back, I answered with trembling hands, my heart pounding in my chest.

Immediately her voice, rich with emotion, reverberated through the line. It struck a resonant chord deep within me; it had been five long, excruciating years since I had last heard that familiar sound. She was sobbing.

"My son, I am so sorry for everything." There was a pause, and I could picture her looking out the window, perhaps reminiscing or searching for the right words of apology. "I wish I had been there for you when you were leaving. Regardless, I pray each day for your happiness and success. When I heard the news, I was taken by surprise, but it brought me such joy as well."

I could sense the miles between us dwindling as she spoke. Then, she talked to my father after he got on the line too. Their conversation demonstrated the love and support they held for each other, reminding me of the bond they still shared despite the distance and their history.

Before the call concluded, I felt determined to ensure our connection remained strong. I asked Dani to jot down my phone number for my mother and offered to assist her in acquiring a reliable phone. I longed for the moment when we could communicate freely, bridging the gap that time and circumstances had created.

For over a year, she would reach out to me while I was living in Denver. She called me from various numbers to circumvent the barriers that had long separated us, which was usually the fact that she never had a working phone number for very long. Gradually, our conversations blossomed, and I was eager to learn more about her life. I began to ask her deeper questions, still driven by a desire to understand her better and the journey she had taken during our time apart. Each shared story unveiled pieces of her world.

I asked whether she still struggled with alcohol.

Her voice was tinged with weariness when she responded honestly, "Son, I am still drinking; I just cannot seem to stop. To get by, I wash people's clothes to earn a little money."

Hearing her confess this truth concerned me. I asked

where she was living now.

"I am staying with family," she said, naming the members.

But when I heard the names, I was confused. "These people are strangers to you. Now you are calling them family?"

"Yes, they are related to me."

It was baffling to me to learn she was now residing with strangers who turned out to be her relatives. I wasn't able to connect the dots of her stories fast enough.

"But why are you staying there? I thought you were living somewhere else with other family members."

"That situation became unstable, so I had to leave."

The instability of her situation weighed heavily on my heart. She seemed to frequently move to escape escalating conflicts with the people she lived with. It was hard to tell exactly what the conflicts were about because she only told me that she was not wanted there, or that they had a fight over something silly. She would never elaborate. Each shift in her living situation was a reminder to me of her precarious existence. I couldn't ask her who was to blame when her situation turned unstable. I could only speculate.

Worried about her well-being, I urged her to seek out her actual relatives in The Gambia or Bissau, the country she originally called home.

"Ugh," she sighed into the phone. "I have no immediate family left, and I do not want to relocate to Bissau."

Why is this woman suffering? Why is this happening to

her? My mother's words were of uncertainty and fear, yet in this turmoil, our renewed communication sparked a fragile hope that we could rebuild our relationship despite the vast distance and challenges we faced. I felt that maybe once I was financially established in the United States, I could fly back to help her in person.

Driven by a desire to understand her struggles better, I shifted my focus to her ongoing battle with alcohol during our phone calls. I felt an urgent need to grasp why she continued to drink and what had led her down this dark path in the first place. However, every time I approached the sensitive subject, my mother would become defensive, her demeanor tightening like a drawn curtain.

She would bristle at my concern, responding with an intensity that shocked me. "I was drinking before you were born; nobody was able to stop me. Who do you think you are to tell me to stop drinking?" Her confrontational tone shot through me, leaving annoyance simmering in my chest, yet it also fueled my determination to help her conquer her addiction. I resolved to do whatever it took to support her journey toward sobriety.

My mother's excessive alcohol consumption meant that she was frequently inebriated, even during our phone calls, and this created a frustrating and painful dynamic between us. Conversations that should have been meaningful and nurturing often devolved into confusion and irritation. It felt as though I was entering a minefield each time I rang her up;

approaching her while she was drunk resulted in her complete inability to recall our discussions. Any important words I tried to convey were misconstrued or lost in the haze of her intoxication.

On the rare occasions when she was sober, I would gather my courage to speak honestly with her, only to be met with her dismissal. It was as if my words were mere whispers in a bustling crowd—listened to but ignored—leaving me feeling powerless and unheard.

CHAPTER ELEVEN

By 2015, I had found my place in Aurora, Colorado, but continued to see my father on a regular basis. As the year went on and I continued with the challenges of living on my own and working in the United States, I received the heartbreaking news that my beloved Baba had fallen gravely ill. He had struggled with diabetes, and it seemed that the grip of the disease had finally caught up with him.

On December 15th of that year, the world grew dimmer as he passed away. This moment was profoundly painful for me. An ache settled deep in my heart and soul. He was not only my grandfather but also my mentor, the one individual who truly understood the depth of my struggles and my emotions. Even though he was no longer here, the essence of his memory coursed through me, weaving through my thoughts and presence, reminding me of all that we shared. But with his departure from Earth, a sense of loneliness enveloped me, leaving me feeling lost and devastated. This was only made worse by the fact that I was unable to return to The Gambia for any services held for him.

All the emotional turmoil I had been under began to manifest physically, taking a toll on my health, a clear indicator of the persistent stress weighing on my mind and body. Despite these mounting signs of my suffering, I felt trapped in silence. There were days when I craved nothing more than to retreat into the comfort of my Colorado home, pulling the curtains closed to shut out the outside world, and surrender myself to sleep.

In those moments, I was trapped by the heaviness of my mother's struggles and my grandfather's death. Deep down, I knew I needed help, but my stubbornness convinced me that I could shoulder all the burdens alone.

In my quest to find relief from the daily strain, I read books and watched funny YouTube videos, yet the mere act of beginning anything felt overwhelming. Then, when I least expected it, someone I randomly crossed paths with opened my eyes a bit further.

I often encountered this man at the bus stop on my way to work. He had an easy smile and a genuine curiosity about life. Our conversations meandered from lighthearted banter to deeper topics. One day, I confided in him about the stress I was carrying. He suggested I seek therapy, a concept that felt foreign and almost laughable in my African community. I chuckled dismissively, questioning how sitting down with a therapist could possibly alleviate my complex problems. He pressed on, however, maintaining that it would be to my benefit and I should reconsider it. At the time, I brushed off his advice without comprehending its significance.

Still fueled by a determination to help my mother secure the care she so obviously needed, I realized I had to act with urgency. No matter where she moved, I made a consistent effort to keep her anchored in one place, believing that stability could offer her some comfort. Each time she received money from me, however, it seemed almost instinctive for her to pack her bags and vanish again. Feeling the responsibility, I reached out to the people she was staying with, offering more financial support to ensure they would encourage her to remain in one place and prioritize her well-being.

I took additional precautions, even stopping her from taking in people's laundry for extra money. It became clear to me that it was time for me to bear the full responsibility for her care. My heart ached for her; she had faced her struggles alone for far too long, and I knew that sending money to take care of everything she needed wasn't enough. In my desperate quest to help my mother break free from the suffocating grip of alcohol, I needed to explore all avenues that might aid her. But how would I be able to help her from so far away and while dealing with struggles of my own? I felt I was gasping for air while swimming in a storm.

Soon my mother called me to tell me she had chosen to move in with a close-knit group of friends once again. I was surprised by my reaction to this news. I was calm. I had grown accustomed to her constant relocations. In the past, her moves would infuriate me, each relocation fueling my frustration at having to send money through new strangers with each move. However, this time, an unsettling sense of helplessness filled me. I felt like a spectator in my mother's life, resigned to the idea that I had no choice but to accept her decisions. A new and complex mix of emotions took hold of me.

One bright afternoon, a few days after her call, I engaged in a heartfelt conversation with my mother's friend Mariama. She spoke candidly about her deep concerns regarding the alcohol addiction, expressing genuine worry that something was fundamentally amiss within her. "I am very worried about your mother's drinking, John. It appears to be more than just a habit; something deeper is driving her to seek solace in a bottle, and it's clearly taking a toll on her emotional well-being."

"I sense that sometimes, too, but it's excruciatingly hard to watch her spiral like this. It leaves me with a heavy feeling of anger and helplessness," I confessed, my heart burdened with her struggles.

"Try not to let anger fuel your feelings, my son. Understand that what she is facing is her own personal battle, one that she is grappling with in silence. It's crucial to offer her compassion instead of judgment," Mariama advised, her tone calm yet nurturing, as if she were trying to guide me through this emotional storm.

"You are right, Mariama. But I seriously need to figure out how to be there for her, even when it feels like an uphill battle." Our discussion ended on a hopeful note.

A few days later, I picked up the phone to call my mother again.

"Hello?" It was Mariama who answered, not my mother.

"How are you, Mariama? And where is my mom? What is she up to?"

"John, she has decided to convert to Islam."

My heart jolted. It felt as though I had stepped into an alternate reality, and my mind spun as I tried to comprehend this unexpected turn of events. "Could you repeat that, please?"

Mariama kindly reassured me. "My son, your mother needs God right now."

Apprehension and curiosity rippled through me. "Please hand the phone to my mother."

"Hello, John."

I greeted her and asked about the conversion. "Is this true?"

To my astonishment, my mother confirmed her genuine desire to embrace Islam. "Yes. This new belief will be a significant change for me and will help me triumph over my long-standing struggle with alcohol dependency." Each word she uttered resonated with deep sincerity, and I could hear a palpable sense of relief in her voice.

"Okay, if this is what you need, I will try to support it." Something remarkable shifted within me; for the first time in what felt like an eternity, a concrete glimmer of hope ignited in my chest—perhaps this change could indeed guide my mother toward the healing she so desperately needed. But still, this news was accompanied by a whirlwind of emotions that came at me from both sides of the issue.

My mother handed the phone back to Mariama.

"Mariama, I have mixed thoughts about my mother's conversion to Islam. I really need to seek understanding."

"John, it will all be okay, I assure you."

Once the call ended, I was left grappling with my conflicting feelings—part of me was sad, while another part sparkled with a cautious joy. The sadness stemmed from my strong Catholic upbringing, which made it challenging for me to fully embrace my mother's choice to convert.

A heavy weight settled in my heart, knowing I couldn't persuade her to reconsider her path. Yet, in this emotional storm, I clung to the hope that perhaps this new chapter in her life would finally lead her to cease drinking—a habit that seemed to poison her existence for too long.

As I thought about the situation, it became increasingly apparent that my mother was genuinely seeking a spiritual connection, one that I hoped Islam would offer her, providing the support and guidance she needed to heal and rebuild her life anew.

Despite my not believing in Islam, many of my relatives

had embraced the religion, and I admired how they remained steadfast in their beliefs. Growing up, I also had numerous cousins who were raised in the traditions of Islam, and I enjoyed forming deep, meaningful friendships with many wonderful Muslim individuals.

In the midst of my worries about my mother's decision, a small part of me found solace. At least she will have faith and a connection to God. I believed that with divine guidance, she might finally discover the strength she needed to overcome her challenges.

One afternoon, I gathered my courage to call my mother and check on her. However, things with my mother were not as they seemed, once again.

CHAPTER TWELVE

My mother announced that she could no longer practice Islam. Another jolt of disbelief hit me. My heart began to race, confusion and concern flooding my mind as I pressed her for details. "Mother, what is going on? What is the reason behind this sudden change? It has only been a few weeks since you told me you were converting. What happened?"

"John, you are just a kid."

I was in my mid-twenties.

"You don't understand anything about life. I have lost interest, and I am leaving this house right now."

My stomach clenched up. "What are you planning to do? Where will you go?"

"I will call you back…" She hung up.

A few days later, she left me a message that she had moved to a small town called Bara, not far from Banjul, the capital of The Gambia. I couldn't shake the realization that her constant relocations were steadily eroding her health, both physically and emotionally. With each move, I became increasingly anxious about her safety, worrying that something might happen to her. Would this vicious cycle ever end?

I approached my father, seeking his help in bringing her closer to us. "Could we arrange for her to stay with our family in Lamin?" At my grandparents' house, she could be with my siblings and stepmother."

My father, understanding the seriousness of the situation, agreed to take action. "I will reach out to your mother and discuss a plan for her return to the family home. She will not have to lift a finger—no cooking or laundry—everything would be taken care of."

At first, my mother seemed receptive to the idea, which momentarily eased my spirits. However, knowing her history of honoring commitments, I remained cautiously optimistic.

Days later, and true to her nature, my mother changed her mind, completely denying that she had made any agreement with my father, my stepmother, and me. This didn't surprise me in the least.

Respectfully accepting her decision without pressing her further, we began to explore alternative arrangements. We found her a modest place to stay, not too far from our home in Lamin.

She settled there for a time, and I set out on my own quest, working diligently to purchase some land in The Gambia where I could build her a more stable and secure home, one that would truly be hers. Eventually, I was able to arrange to purchase a plot of land and began to draw up plans to build her a home.

However, a couple months later, I was informed that my mother had moved yet again, this time to stay nearby with a relative named Babtin.

One day, Babtin reached out to me. "Your mother is still drinking heavily. We need to take urgent action. I know of a man in another village who is an expert at resolving this sort of problem."

I didn't even ask Babtin to delve into the details of how this process worked because I was only interested in whether it would help my mother. "How much would it cost to get you to take my mother to this man? I am willing to cover all necessary expenses."

When she provided me with the amount, I immediately sent the money. To my relief, my mother responded positively to the plan. When she and Babtin received my funds, they set off for the village to get to this man.

Over the years, I had gathered that deep down, my mother genuinely wanted to stop drinking. She would often express her desire to quit, but then described alcohol as her coping mechanism.

I would ask her, "Coping with what?" She would only elaborate on her feelings of loneliness and the hardships she had endured in life, but not much beyond that. And I didn't ask further out of respect.

Still, I was keen to assist her, and I believed that freeing her from the grasp of alcohol would fundamentally change her. I envisioned that without alcohol, we could engage in meaningful conversations, fostering a healthier relationship. However, the reality was more complicated.

My mother often exhibited anger and frustration when she was sober. Conversely, she was more approachable when she was drinking, but having a serious dialogue with her during those times was futile—once intoxicated, she would forget our discussions altogether.

When my mother and Babtin returned from the village after spending time with the expert, her life underwent a significant transformation. She managed to abstain from alcohol and did not drink. Yet, despite this positive change, things took a troubling turn as my mother moved several times again. It was evident she struggled to maintain her relationships with relatives, and the reasons for these conflicts were complex and delicate. I needed to work harder and faster on the home I wanted to build for her. However, it was difficult residing in the United States while trying to start with the construction details so far away in The Gambia.

Before we broke ground, I was able to locate a decent apartment for her to stay in until the new house was complete. This place had access to electricity and running water.

After she had settled there, I began to plan how to build that perfect home for her, hoping to provide her with a more permanent living arrangement. However, as time elapsed and even though she had stopped drinking, our relationship worsened.

Our interactions were characterized by constant disputes, and I found it incredibly challenging to support her in any capacity. My mother was resistant to living with anyone, and every suggestion I made—like bringing in a caregiver—was met with refusal; she likely perceived such gestures as attempts to control her life. Even when I asked my siblings to buy her some cute home decor and fun accessories to make her living space more inviting, she would often react with anger, sometimes refusing to even acknowledge or accept the gifts.

During phone calls with my siblings, who would pass on information about my mother to me, and also calls from my mother herself, where she would often complain about everything going on, I found that her mental health was deteriorating. She exhibited even more erratic behavior. Some days she seemed fine, enjoying her independence, while other days she was engulfed in a dark cloud of despair. The drastic fluctuations in her mood were concerning, and I longed for the loving, understanding relationship we sometimes shared, but it seemed to slip further and further away with each passing day.

The intense mood swings occurred multiple times throughout the day. I began to suspect she might be dealing with withdrawals. The healthcare system in The Gambia, unfortunately, was severely lacking, and left me anxious about whether she would receive the necessary medical attention and assistance. I felt lost and overwhelmed, scrambling to figure out how to help her from so far away, all while struggling with my own emotions and establishing my own life in Denver.

I was unable to confide in anyone about the distressing situation. The fear of judgment was large in my mind—not only for me but also for my mother. In African society, there is a tendency to talk openly about problems, yet very little tangible help is ever provided. Especially when facing mental health issues, there is a significant stigma attached, which often leads to these challenges being ignored, downplayed, normalized, and minimized. Despite witnessing my mother's struggles, I even found myself falling into a state of denial about the severity of her condition. I was not ready to fully accept what was unfolding before me. Every morning, I woke up with the hope that things might start to change for the better.

I decided to reach out to a cherished friend named Khadijah, who felt like a biological sister to me. She resided in the United Kingdom, and over the years, she had become a steadfast pillar of support in my life. "Sis, I've been grappling with so much concerning my mother, and I just need someone to talk to."

"You can always confide in me about anything that is weighing you down," Khadijah said, her voice resonating with empathy and reassurance.

As I recounted the emotional turmoil and distress I was experiencing, Khadijah listened intently, her understanding silence offering solace. Once I finished, she took a moment to gather her thoughts before replying, "In this world, everything happens for a reason. Trust that God is in control and keep your faith strong. You must remember that there is a purpose in your struggles. I am here for you, always. If you ever need someone to talk to or seek guidance from, I'll be right by your side. And you know what? I would like to involve my mother in this, too; she has a remarkable gift for helping those who are navigating their own storms."

This heartfelt conversation signaled another turning point in my life. Khadijah not only became a source of comfort but also emerged as a guiding light, illuminating my path during a difficult chapter. Her unwavering support reminded me that even in my darkest moments, it was okay to express my own struggles, and that I was not alone in facing my challenges.

Khadijah's mother lived in The Gambia near my mother and played a significant and compassionate role in my mother's life, reaching out to her during difficult times and fostering an unexpected but meaningful friendship. It warmed my heart to witness how someone could bring a level of stability into my mother's world.

Khadijah's mother had a unique gift for building connections; she would regularly invite my mother to spend the night at her home, especially during important Muslim festive occasions like Koriteh and Tobaski. With deep religious significance, these were opportunities to show gratitude, obedience, and remembrance of faith, as well as occasions to visit family and friends, share food, and dress beautifully. I was glad my mother was able to take part in these shared traditions that fostered much-needed laughter, happiness, and community.

Khadijah's mother possessed a remarkable ability to soothe my mother's anxieties and restore her sense of calm, employing a gentle and reassuring approach that lightened my mother's mood and created an atmosphere of peace.

I couldn't demonstrate enough how much I owed Khadijah and her mother, not only for supporting my mother but also for supporting me. They always listened without judgment, understanding the unique challenges I faced. Whenever I felt hopeless, they provided words of encouragement and consolation. Their kindness created a safe space for me to explore and express my feelings.

CHAPTER THIRTEEN

In March 2021, I made the important decision to buy a plane ticket and visit my mother, as she was scheduled for a medical procedure. It had been over a decade since I last saw her. While taking time off from classes and using paid time off from work, I lived through each moment leading up to the visit in a surreal state of mind. I daydreamed about how our reunion would transpire, picturing us embracing, tears of joy in our eyes as we finally reconnected. I envisioned us sharing stories about our lives, reminiscing about the past, and rebuilding the bond that had been strained by time, distance, and circumstances.

In my efforts to make this trip even more special, I invited my half-sister Neneth from Senegal. She agreed, but could only join me a few days after my arrival. I hoped that when the three of us were together, we could create a loving atmosphere. I imagined cooking traditional meals, sharing happy memories, and simply enjoying each other's company, all of which would contribute to healing not just for our mother but for our entire family.

This trip felt pivotal, offering the warmth and love I longed for, and it seemed to hold the promise of mending the emotional gaps left by years of separation. As my departure date drew closer, my anticipation grew. I couldn't help but wonder what state my mother would be in. Would she be feeling fragile, or perhaps have a moment of clarity? What were her current preferences and dislikes? Would the words between us flow comfortably?

I boarded the plane from the United States to The Gambia. After a very long journey, I finally landed and breathed in the familiar air. I was so happy. My younger brother, Amzo—born of Greg's other marriage—and my dear friend Wally, welcomed me with open arms at the airport, their faces radiating joy, which soothed my anxious spirit.

Following our family tradition, we made our way to my family home first. This was an age-old ritual that I wanted to uphold, but it also meant I couldn't go straight to my mother's apartment just yet.

By the time we arrived at my family's home, the sky had turned deep blue and the stars were sparkling. Although my mother's apartment remained out of reach for the night, the warmth of my siblings surrounded me.

"How is life in the United States?" Amzo inquired, his voice filled with genuine curiosity as he studied my face.

"You look different now."

"America is truly wonderful! And yes, I've let my beard grow, which definitely gives me a new look, haha."

Amzo laughed along with me, his eyes gleaming with delight.

"You all have changed so much, too! I'm really thrilled to be here with everyone again," I said. "I am looking forward to the wonderful moments we will create together in the days to come."

After our brief conversation, with a sense of anticipation bubbling inside me, I called my mother. "I will be there to see you first thing in the morning."

I sensed her relief on the other end of the line. She said, "I appreciate knowing you are on your way."

The following morning, I sprang into action. Amzo decided to join me, and together we set out for my mother's apartment.

"Mother," I said, my voice like a wispy cloud leaving my body.

"John, you are here, finally." She wrapped her arms around me, and it was like a dream to embrace her again after all this time, and the sheer happiness radiating from her face mirrored my own emotions.

She led us into her living room. Her smile illuminated the house, transforming the space into a warm haven of love and nostalgia—a moment I wanted to etch into my memory forever. My mother's apartment was a testament to her care and attention to detail. The space was carefully arranged, creating an inviting atmosphere with a sense of hominess. A sleek flat-screen TV framed by a stunning glossy stand stood prominently against the wall, drawing the eye with its modern elegance. Next to it, a stylish stand fan whirred, its gentle hum providing a refreshing breeze.

Once we settled in, my mother called Khadijah's mother to come over. I could hardly contain my excitement; I was eager for the chance to finally meet her in person.

When Khadijah's mother arrived, the electric atmosphere that was swirling within me calmed. The conversation flowed effortlessly, and it warmed my heart to see my mother engaging so positively with her friend and neighbor. For a couple of precious hours, we shared what had happened in our lives.

As darkness settled in, I sensed the air in the room shift—like a sudden storm obscuring a clear sky. I feared this reunion might be the only pleasant time I would share with my mother before my departure back to the United States. I didn't want it to end. I tried to push the thought to the back of my mind.

Perhaps I wasn't the only one who felt a shift. Within a few minutes, someone suggested we all venture out to Lamin to spend the rest of the evening with family at my grandfather's house.

We managed to get to Lamin without any bickering, and everyone seemed relatively happy and at peace. The entire family gathered around the big table, and plates of food appeared. We ate, we conversed, we laughed. After about an hour, my body told me it was exhausted. I needed a moment alone to gather my emotions and give my heart and head a rest. For the past day, I had been going from grateful to anxious, back to calm, then frenetic again. I just needed an empty room so I could process my thoughts. I went down the hall to my aunt's room and sat on the edge of the bed. I took a few deep breaths.

After several minutes, one of my siblings knocked on the door. "John, I don't mean to shock you, but your mother just got up and left in a fit of anger."

My heart sank in confusion. "What did she get upset about?"

"No one here knows why."

I rushed into the main room. "Amzo, come with me, we will try to find her," I said, as everyone's blank faces looked at me, stunned.

We headed to my mother's place. I asked Amzo to wait outside and give me a chance to talk to her first. Stepping into the living room, I was met with a profound silence. There, I found her seated alone, a cloud of distress hanging over her.

Cautiously, I approached. "What happened, Mother?"

She turned away, refusing to meet my gaze and shut me out completely. It felt as if an impenetrable wall had risen between us, and it was one she had built herself.

Amzo then came into the room, his voice low and cautionary. "John, I need to remind you of your mother's tendency to spiral into anger without any clear reason."

I turned to face him. "I have long been aware of her patterns." But my heart wrestled with denial, unwilling to accept the reality of the moment. I had traveled all this way, across continents, to see her, and for what? For this? For her to shut down and look at a wall instead of communicating with me?

In the days leading up to my trip, I discovered that my mother's scheduled hospital procedure had been postponed, adding a heavy layer of stress to her already complicated life. With the Easter holiday coinciding with my visit, I had hoped it would serve as a chance for our family to come together and find comfort in one another's company. I mustered the courage to ask her if she would join everyone in Lamin to celebrate Easter in a few days.

"I prefer to celebrate the Easter Feast alone in my own home," she said to the wall.

While I had to respect her choice, I felt compelled to express my intentions. "Well, I still plan to see my siblings on Easter Day, even if just for a brief visit. I want to uphold these vital family connections. All I am trying to do is find a way to balance my desire to support you with my commitment to our family traditions."

She was unmoved by what I said, and after what seemed

like the longest moment, Amzo touched my shoulder and motioned that we should leave.

CHAPTER FOURTEEN

Three days before Easter, with the sun shining brightly, I made my way to Lamin to attend the church services alongside my siblings. The day brimmed with anticipation; the air fragrant with the promise of spring. But as evening fell, my night took an unsettling turn when the phone rang.

"John, I am a neighbor of your mother. Did you know she just left her house? She said she was going traveling now. I'm wondering if you know where she is going?"

My heart lurched into my throat, and I gasped, "Traveling?"

"Yes, that's what she said."

"Did she say for how long?"

"Well, that's why I'm calling you. And the thing is, your mother appeared quite upset as she was leaving."

A cascade of concern washed over me, fueling a growing sense of urgency. After hanging up with the neighbor, I attempted to call my mother's cell phone, but to my dismay, my calls went unanswered; each ring ended in deafening silence. Something was amiss, and with each passing minute, the weight of uncertainty pressed down harder, draining any hope of what should have been a joyful time.

I somehow managed to sleep through the night, even with all the stress. The following day, I attempted to call my mother again.

"Hello?" she finally answered.

"Mother, where are you? Why did you go?" I was relieved to be talking to her.

"I left to visit relatives for the Feast and won't be returning home anytime soon."

"What?" How could she leave without addressing the storm of issues between us? She knew I was only here for a short amount of time, and she was wasting every day, every minute. As I wrestled with my emotions, searching for the right words to convey my feelings, she spoke up.

"You don't want to be with me."

Those words felt like a knife piercing my heart, rendering me speechless. She unleashed a torrent of grievances that delved straight into the very core of our relationship—each complaint a painful reminder of our unresolved conflicts.

Her words were far too painful for me to commit to memory, even in the solitude of my thoughts. I knew I couldn't and wouldn't ever share them with anyone.

But still desperate to salvage our connection, I pleaded with her to reconsider and come back home.

"I have made my decision. I am staying here," she said.

Just when I thought she would hang up on me, a relative from her so-called family took the phone from her.

"What kind of son are you?" The woman's voice dripped with disdain. "You told her that you traveled all the way to The Gambia to see her, your sick mother, yet you've been mistreating her this whole time you've been here? Your mother is rightly angry. You need to stay close to her, not abandon her."

Her words reverberated in my mind, amplifying my guilt. Anger pulsed through me, unexpected and fierce. I felt a burning need to defend myself. "Ma'am, I do not know you, and you have no idea what really happened between my mother and me. You created an opinion without listening to the full story. But I will not sit here and justify myself to you over the phone."

The woman brushed off my words, dismissing me as if I were inconsequential. "So says you. Who are you in the first place?"

Determined to mend the growing rift and to at least bring this argument back to a neutral area, I gently promised them that I would call back later.

Fortunately, Uncle Jose was also back in The Gambia and close by at that moment. He asked me to give him the phone. I trusted Uncle Jose completely; he was the one person who could live through a complex and fraught situation like this and come out the other end level-headed. He was someone who could help persuade my mother to reconsider her stance.

However, as the phone went from my hand to Jose's hand, I heard a click on the other end of the line, and I knew she had hung up.

I called my father, who was still in Denver, and relayed the whole incident to him, hoping he could act as a mediator and lend some support. He told me he would get in touch with my mother right away.

About an hour later, however, my father called me back and told me his conversation had spiraled into an argument, only intensifying the turmoil. I felt crushed, as if the weight of the world were pressing down on my shoulders.

On Easter Monday, Uncle Jose stepped in again, his calming presence a stark contrast to the chaos that had been crushing me. With his kind but firm demeanor, he took it upon himself to try to speak with my mother a second time. He picked up my phone, and as he dialed her number, I walked outside to the yard so I wouldn't be able to hear the conversation, should it go awry again. I leaned against the outside wall of the porch, only hearing a few of Jose's muffled words coming through the window, and I waited impatiently, the seconds stretching into what felt like an eternity.

Through an unexpected blend of empathy and authority, however, Jose managed to break through my mother's defenses and persuade her to come home. A sense of hope blossomed within me. She had agreed to return to see me.

A few days later, my wonderful sister Neneth arrived at

our home, instantly infusing the space with warmth and relief. Although our mother wasn't here yet, my sister's presence helped me calm down.

We talked for hours. I recounted every detail of the turmoil that the past few days had led to. I left out nothing of our mother's outburst; my voice sometimes trembled.

As I spoke, my sister listened intently, her gaze fixed and her expression one of stunned silence, as she processed just how heavy my words were.

"Something is definitely wrong with our mother," I said. "It's like her emotions shift in an instant. One moment she's happy, and the next she's angry, her mood darkening without any warning or explanation."

"Yes." Neneth let out a frustrated sigh.

My shoulders slumped. "It makes matters even more difficult when she doesn't tell us what we did wrong; we're left in the dark, desperately trying to decipher her feelings."

Neneth nodded. "I really don't think it's anything you did. The truth is, she can be an incredibly challenging person to interact with, and her unpredictable mood swings often seem completely disconnected from our behavior."

Later on, we made the heartfelt decision to call our mother, eager for her to engage directly with my sister. I sat and listened to Neneth speak with her.

"Are you coming home now?" Neneth asked. The yearning in her tone revealed just how profoundly she also missed the comforting presence of the person on the other end of the line.

"Alright, we'll be here waiting for you," she continued, her eyes sparkling with hope. "We can't wait to see you soon," she added, each syllable infused with the promise of reunion.

The burdensome tension from the past few days began to melt away. That moment reassured me that, despite the storm we had weathered, the bond we shared was unbreakable. There would always be a path leading us back to one another.

The following day, another one of my mother's neighbors—someone I barely knew but who had consistently shown kindness to me—called me with the news that my mother was back home and no longer at the so-called relative's house. Excitement surged through me, making my heart race, as I knew my mother was honoring the plan she and Neneth had made the previous day.

Accompanied by Uncle Jose, Neneth and I went to my mother's house. We sat in a taxi in silence. Everyone was tense. When we finally arrived, the three of us approached the door. To my dismay, it was closed. I thought for sure she would leave it ajar, signaling to us that she was awaiting our arrival and to walk right in. But this closed door was an unwelcome barrier. We tried the door handle. It was locked. We knocked, our fists echoing against the metallic door.

Uncle Jose called out to my mother.

"Mother!" Neneth and I both shouted.

"I've brought them here to see you," Jose added. "Please

come to the door."

We hoped to coax her into opening the door. But silence greeted us instead, a heavy, oppressive stillness that left me feeling both worried and helpless. Resigned to the reality that we had subconsciously known all along but couldn't acknowledge until this moment, the three of us left.

CHAPTER FIFTEEN

The following day, Neneth, Jose, and I ventured back to my mother's house to try again. This time the door was unlocked, and my mother welcomed us with a bright smile, her mood noticeably lighter than the days before. None of us felt it was worth asking about the locked door. Why derail the reunion now that it was finally happening?

I watched my mother's expression as she took in Neneth. Witnessing their reunion after nearly two decades was overwhelming for all of us, and my eyes grew misty. This was a moment they both had long anticipated—we all had been. They shared a heartfelt embrace; I could feel my mother's genuine happiness radiating as she held her daughter close.

"My dearest child, it feels like an eternity since we have been together. I can hardly believe that the moment I've yearned for has finally arrived," my mother said, her voice quivering.

My sister beamed with emotion, her heart full as she

replied, "I've dreamed of this moment too for so many years. The ache of missing you has been a constant in my heart."

To my delight, my mother then said she wanted to call her sister, who lived in Dakar, Senegal, and share the news of my visit. I nodded that it would be wonderful.

On the phone, my mother said, "Tani, my son has visited from the United States. Please come in a few days so you can get to know each other."

My aunt arrived a few days later, and it felt like a precious opportunity to connect with someone from my maternal side of the family, someone I had only heard stories about.

With all of us in the same place, we decided it would be a show of great support if we accompanied my mother to her doctor's appointments. I cherished the feeling of our little family gathering. Life felt almost idyllic.

However, the vicious pattern continued, and a dense fog of tension began to settle over our closeness. Barely a week before my scheduled departure back to the United States, a heated argument erupted between my mother and her younger sister Tani. The air crackled with unresolved emotions, and what had begun as a simple disagreement about a matter that I really couldn't identify, escalated very quickly. My aunt left the house without saying another word, feeling unwelcome and hurt.

In the aftermath, my mother's demeanor transformed dramatically. The warmth she had shown me faded like the last light of day, and soon she was outside venting to the neighbors about personal matters. I stood watching her from the front door, bewildered and betrayed, struggling to grasp the reasons behind this hurtful and repetitive shift.

Later, when I was at her place, she suddenly told me, "Leave my home and return to Lamin."

I was torn between my loyalty to my mother and my need for distance from her. "I won't leave you. I am going to stay here." I found my voice, and the decision came to my mind. I wasn't going to comply with her wishes. This only added to her fury.

She unleashed a cascade of hurtful claims. "You prefer your stepmother, siblings, and your father's relatives over me."

"Yes, I came to visit you, but I also need to see my siblings. I missed them too. That is why I go there to spend some time and nights there."

She did not respond, and I was finally compelled to make a different choice. "I will leave now."

That confrontation marked another painful low point in our relationship.

I stepped out of the compound, the hot afternoon air hitting my face as tears streamed down my cheeks, blurring my vision. As I reached Lamin, I spotted a secluded room tucked away from the bustling street. I closed the door behind me with a soft click and allowed my emotions to flood out.

I sobbed, releasing the hurt of my mother's constant

rejection and the unpredictable rollercoaster that shaped our relationship. It felt as if I were drowning in my grief, lost in a sea of unresolved feelings.

I attempted to gather myself and left the room. Despite what was going on inside me, I tried to maintain a semblance of composure around my friends and neighbors, hiding the turmoil. It was a struggle.

One afternoon, while I wandered through the colorful stalls of a bustling market, I heard someone call my name. Initially, it didn't register to me that someone familiar to me was calling me. I was so engrossed in my own cloud of sorrow that I couldn't even turn around to see who was there.

"John, John, over here! Hey, John!"

I did eventually turn around to see a friend of mine from Denver, and suddenly remembered that he had told me previously he too would be in The Gambia visiting family at the same time. When he approached me, concern etched across his face from my lack of response.

I finally came to the present moment and acknowledged his presence. Our interaction felt significantly different from our usual cheerful exchanges back in the United States. Instead of sharing laughter and lighthearted banter, he looked straight into my eyes, searching for signs of my well-being.

"Are you okay?" he asked, his gaze piercing through the façade of my brave face. His genuine concern struck me like a cold splash of water, revealing how my pain was manifesting to those around me.

"I am okay; I am just tired. The time change has me exhausted."

I think he knew I wasn't truthful with him, because a few days later, I was surprised when he reached out to my uncle Patrick, expressing worry about my condition. My uncle tried to assuage my friend by backing up my story of exhaustion due to the time change.

Although I tried to maintain a brave front in public, when I found myself alone, my mind was bombarded with anxious thoughts about my mother's health and behavior. Those worries often became too heavy to bear, and I would succumb to tears, seeking solace in the cathartic release of crying. But clearly, I wasn't hiding all this turmoil as well as I thought. My friend sensed it within a few seconds while standing with me near a noisy street vendor.

CHAPTER SIXTEEN

As my time in The Gambia was coming to an end and my departure day approached, I woke up in my mother's cozy apartment, shrouded in a sleepy haze. I still had a long list of things I wanted to do while here. My plan was to fly out the following day, giving me this last day to process the impending goodbye.

After rushing through last-minute shopping and collecting my COVID-19 test result, I returned home, eager to share with my mother that my test was negative. I found her sitting in the living room.

"Hello, Mother!"

She didn't say anything to me, ignoring my attempt at connection. And she wouldn't make eye contact either, actively avoiding any interaction with me.

I could hear dishes and silverware clinking in the kitchen as Neneth busied herself with food preparations, completely unaware of the emotional storm brewing just one room over.

"Okay…" I didn't want to shut my mother out like she was doing to me, but I also didn't want to stand there and let her continue treating me like this. "I think I will go over to Lamin now," I said.

I left my mother's house, hoping for a more inviting atmosphere elsewhere. As I walked through the lively streets, a gnawing sense of urgency seeped into my mind. My heart raced, thumping against my chest as a feeling of unease settled in my gut. It suddenly struck me: I needed to confirm my travel plans for the upcoming flight.

In a rush, I dialed the vendor who had sold me my ticket. Each ring on the other end of the line amplified my anxiety before the call went through.

"Hello, I would like to confirm a flight," I said, then gave my confirmation number.

"Oh, yes, sir, we need to inform you that due to unexpected scheduling changes, you are now set to depart today, not tomorrow."

Panic surged through me like ice water in my veins as I realized I had only two hours left.

In a frenzy, I flung open the door to my grandfather's house and ran to the bedroom, calling out to my relatives with each hurried step.

"Terrible news, you won't believe it. I just found out that my flight leaves today! I have to leave very soon!"

In the bedroom, I flung open my suitcase, carelessly

cramming all my belongings inside. Clothes tangled together in a chaotic pile of wrinkled, clean garments and worn, dirty ones. I grabbed my phone and jabbed out my sister's number. I needed to tell her and my mother right away.

Neneth answered, and I rambled on about what exactly was happening. My voice trembled as I explained my need to get to the airport within the limited time I had, so limited that I wouldn't be able to come back to our mother's house to say goodbye in person—not at all how I wanted the end of this trip to go.

"John," Neneth said, "I am stunned by this news, but I offer you prayers and blessings for safe travels." She provided a small glimmer of comfort.

"Can I talk to Mother? I would like to tell her goodbye."

I heard Neneth call out for our mother. There was no response. Once again, the silence stung more than words could convey—my mother's unwillingness to engage with me was a heavy weight in my chest.

"John—"

My sister didn't need to make an excuse. I knew exactly why our mother wasn't coming to the phone. "It's okay, Neneth, I have to go now. But this trip has meant so much to me. You have no idea."

"Oh, but I do, brother, I do."

After we hung up, I hastily applied deodorant, knowing I would have to skip my evening shower. I picked up the suitcase with one hand and awkwardly hugged my relatives with my free arm.

I raced out of the house toward the airport, only a thirty-minute journey away. To my surprise, I arrived just in the nick of time, though the chaotic rush had left me breathless and disoriented. As I settled into the terminal, my mind was still clouded with worry for my mother.

As the plane ascended into the sky, and I watched the ground of The Gambia go behind the window shade, relief washed over me; I was momentarily free from my mother's problems. Yet, in that relief lingered a deep sadness, a heavy realization that my mother was still grappling with her own struggles, and I could not shield her from them.

When we touched down at DIA, I took out my phone and dialed my mother's number, my heart racing with the uncertainty of what our conversation might unveil.

"I am so sorry, John." She began our discussion with an unexpected apology. "I am sorry for the rifts that have formed between us over the years. And I acknowledge the silent grievances that have built up like a wall, separating us."

In that heartwarming and vulnerable moment, I mirrored her sentiments. "I have my own feelings of hurt and regret too." I moved to stand out of the way of all the other passengers. I faced the wall, knowing I might cry, and I didn't want dozens of strangers to see. I hoped they were all too consumed with their own busy schedules to even notice me.

My mother and I had a deep, honest dialogue, and we both asked for forgiveness from each other, allowing the burdens of our past to lighten ever so slightly. Each exchanged word, each "I'm sorry," felt like a gentle untying of the knots of tension between us.

By the end of our conversation, I discovered a newfound sense of optimism. I once again dared to believe that this heartfelt exchange might indeed be the signal of a healthier, more harmonious chapter in our relationship—one built on understanding, empathy, and a renewed commitment to each other.

At the beginning of my trip to The Gambia, I had hoped she and I could have this exact conversation in person. But standing there in the bustling airport at the very tail end of my trip, I realized that the only way this conversation would happen was the way *she* needed it to happen.

CHAPTER SEVENTEEN

Shortly after I returned to the United States, I received the harrowing news that my mother's health had taken a dramatic turn for the worse. She was frequently admitted to the hospital, each visit a painful reminder of the fragility of life. I could hardly bear the emotional upheaval of hearing how her condition fluctuated so drastically. She seemed more lost in a fog of confusion, weak and disoriented, crying out for understanding in a world that felt increasingly alien to her. It became evident that her ongoing decline was not just a phase but an irreversible reality that we were all still trying to comprehend.

My thoughts continually drifted back to the pressing need to bring my mother to the United States for a thorough medical evaluation. However, I encountered a huge obstacle that seemed insurmountable: She lacked a birth certificate. This crucial document was not merely a formality; it was essential for her to obtain a visa for travel and to access the medical care she required.

Despite my efforts to weed through the bureaucratic maze surrounding this issue, I faced one frustrating hurdle after another. I scoured government offices, filled out endless forms, and made numerous inquiries, only to be met with red tape and delays.

The situation was especially heartbreaking given the dismal state of the healthcare system in The Gambia, which had inadequate resources and insufficient care options. During my visit, I had witnessed her struggle and the lack of improvement. Her mental and physical states were in fact deteriorating. Time was slipping away, and I needed to find a solution.

In all the turbulence, my mother articulated a profound desire to be baptized, viewing it as a pivotal step toward spiritual rejuvenation. It was a powerful moment—a chance for her to reclaim some semblance of control over her life.

My heart was so heavy because I felt she knew her time was near and that she didn't have much fight left to survive. However, her desire to be baptized gave me a new sense of purpose. I reached out to a priest local to my mother's area, who kindly agreed to perform the ceremony.

I was told that the baptism took place in a serene, quiet setting, surrounded by a few family members. It offered my mother—and me—a deep sense of peace and comfort, a tranquil anchor in the storm of suffering. The ceremony was not just a ritual; it was a moment of grace, a beautiful testament to her enduring spirit and the love that surrounded her. I just wish I could have been there to witness it.

On the somber morning of May 28, 2022, fifteen months after my visit to The Gambia, I received a devastating call from my sister that shattered my world: Our beloved mother had passed away. The news struck me like a tidal wave, leaving my family in sorrow and disbelief.

I could hardly process the reality of her eternal absence. It was as if I were trapped in a nightmare from which I could not awaken. As a result of this tragedy, I reached out to my employer, requesting compassionate leave. They graciously granted my request, allowing me the necessary time to process the depths of my grief and to travel back to The Gambia, where the preparations for my mother's funeral were already underway.

The journey was a blur; each mile felt endless as my heart ached with longing for just one more moment with her. Upon my arrival, I was met by familiar faces—family members and friends united in our shared loss. The funeral itself was heart-wrenching, as we gathered to honor her remarkable life with tears streaming down our faces and poignant memories echoing in the air. The atmosphere was thick with love and sadness, each person thinking about the irreplaceable void her passing had left in our lives.

The evening after the funeral, I cried. I yearned for a

companion, someone who could understand the depth of my grief and engage in heartfelt conversations about her life and legacy, to honor her memory in a meaningful way that absolutely captured the essence of my love and loss.

I was heartbroken, pondering the life she had lived with resilience. I thought deeply about the series of events that had led to this moment and attempted to piece together the precious memories, lessons, and love she had bestowed upon us throughout her life. A powerful sense of determination surged within me to uncover the hidden truth behind my mother's enduring struggles once and for all.

I wanted to speak to my older sister and my aunt, hoping they could shed light on the shadows that cloaked my mother's life and unravel the challenges she had long faced. However, when I broached the subject with my aunt, her response was tinged with reluctance, her posture rigid and defensive, which hinted at a protective instinct within her.

"John, you know how it is, people are just different from what you expect, and you don't always get the life you want. And sometimes life is hard, and you just have to accept that," was her cryptic response.

I tried to dig further, asking about my mother's life before she had me. Aunt Tani alluded to the painful beginnings of my mother's difficulties, rooted in her troubled childhood spent under the harsh scrutiny of her parents. Their cold indifference and lack of support had left scars that followed my mother into her adult life.

Despite my aunt's evident hesitance to delve deeper into those memories, I pressed on, my heart racing. "What do you mean? Tell me what happened."

"Not right now, John. It's been a trying day."

I expressed my desperation to grasp the intricate details of my mother's past, believing that unearthing these buried truths was not just an act of curiosity but a vital step toward my own healing. My yearning for clarity intensified as I recognized that piecing together her story held the key to not only comprehending her struggles but also to fortifying our familial bonds.

My mind was a torrent of memories of her life. Profound questions continued to tug at my heart. Why did she have to endure such an extraordinary amount of suffering, often masked by her gentle smile?

Regret filled me as I pondered what I could have done differently to ease her burdens. Where did I falter as her son, a role I cherished? Did my actions, even if unintentional, cause her pain or heartache? None of this felt right! She deserved a life that contained joy, laughter, and warmth, surrounded by those she loved.

I realized I must confront these emotional struggles head-on. In these moments of introspection and contemplation, I resolved that upon my return to Denver, I would seek to learn more about the profound wisdom and respect my father still had for my mother. I wanted to uncover the hidden layers of her identity. What was she like as a nurturing parent? What was the essence of her being? What were her truest dreams and unfulfilled desires? I longed for my father to recount the enchanting tale of their serendipitous meeting, the spark that ignited the love they shared.

I wanted to understand not just the woman who brought me into this world, but also the person she was before motherhood—a vibrant individual with her own passions and stories. I hoped to learn about the moments that shaped her, the challenges she faced, and the triumphs that defined her. I believed that delving into these personal narratives would illuminate the depths of her soul, granting me a clearer understanding of her complexities and a path toward my own healing.

CHAPTER EIGHTEEN

At the start of 2025, all I could think about was when I could fly back to The Gambia again. This next journey was important to me because I wanted to plan a traditional memorial service for my mother. The event meant a lot to our family; it was a way to honor her life and fulfill her wishes.

In Gambian culture, as in many others across Africa, a funeral service similar to those held in the West takes place after someone dies. However, our culture also believes in celebrating the individual's life in a separate ceremony as well. There is no time frame for when this second celebration should take place, but it must be done at some point. Our belief is that if the second celebration does not happen in due time, the deceased would send signs.

This second celebration was meant to be joyful—full of dancing—rather than somber like the first funeral. Part of this traditional celebration is the sacrifice of a cow or other animal. The elders in the community pour out bottles of alcohol when calling the name of the person being celebrated. My generation, however, sees this as a waste of money and time, but when our parents had requested this tradition while they were alive, we felt we had to abide by their wishes.

In the weeks leading up to the celebratory memorial trip, I took the initiative to purchase my ticket well in advance, affirming my deep commitment to the occasion. I had dedicated to saving money specifically for my mother's memorial and meticulously planned every detail to ensure that each aspect expressed the profound love and respect we had for her.

In an effort to unite our family during this poignant time of mourning and preparation to celebrate her life, I wanted to reach out to several of my mother's relatives. These were relatives who did not attend the first funeral for my mother, and much less than that, I had never met them in person, ever. But, again, to make sure the second celebration followed all customs and traditions, I shared the date of the service in the hope of fostering connections through our shared memories and collective grief.

Seeking guidance, I first went to talk to Jokin, a relative of my mother's who was somewhat older than me and had attended the funeral service. We had a warm relationship with each other and collaborated on the plans for gathering in my mother's honor.

But then Jokin said, "John, I am concerned about your planning. I want you to be aware that you need to consult the elders in your mother's family before proceeding any further."

I was taken aback by his comments; they were so far afield from how everyone else felt. I asked him why.

"As you know, I cannot advise you on what to do with the ceremony since I am not old enough to be considered an elder. I do not have that status in the family, and there's nothing I can do about it. You need to talk to the elders in your mother's family. They have to be the ones to tell you what to do and what not to do."

I had always viewed Jokin as a steady source of support, but now his concerns about my plans left me in a state of confusion, forcing me to reassess my decisions. He felt it was imperative to consult my mother's biological siblings—whom I had never met. He said I couldn't move forward with any arrangements without consulting these elders, a process that was already cumbersome to plan from the United States. In addition, I was only a few weeks from departing for The Gambia.

My mind raced with questions about the opinions of these elders and the potential ramifications. Jokin assured me that he would reach out to them and promised to call me back with their response. Yet, as I awaited his update, I couldn't shake the mounting anxiety, anticipating the complications that might arise.

A few days later, Jokin called back with an unusual request. He asked for my father's phone number.

Instantly, I was hit with curiosity, but it was soon eclipsed by a sense of apprehension. I couldn't help but wonder why he needed to speak with my father, especially considering their sporadic communication history. "I would like some clarity; why would you like to speak with my father? The two of you have not spoken since my mother's funeral."

Jokin offered only vague responses, which only deepened my sense of discomfort. Despite my lingering worries, I ultimately decided to give him my father's number. Perhaps I was overthinking the situation, and there was nothing really to worry about.

"Can I also give you the name and number of another distant relative of mine who lives in Guinea-Bissau?" I said, hoping to alleviate any potential tension and foster goodwill. I hoped that by extending this gesture, I might somehow ease the situation, but I still couldn't shake the feeling that something more complicated was at play.

My father called me from his apartment in Denver. "Some unsettling developments have come to light. During a conversation I had with Jokin, he said his elders demanded a few things that caught me off guard."

As I listened, our family's complicated situation reared its ugly head like never before.

"It is important to adhere to family traditions, particularly when it comes to memorial activities. Your mother's siblings are adamant that before you get to actively participate in any of these ceremonies, you are required to observe specific traditional rituals."

"What do you mean?"

"They warned that neglecting their requests could result in serious spiritual consequences that could impact you. Your well-being and the harmony of our family lineage are in danger here."

"I should speak to Jokin again to get clarification, don't you think?" I wanted to understand not only the nature of these rituals but also their significance within our cultural framework, hoping to grasp the deeper values and beliefs that my family held dear.

"Listen, John, they asked that you and Neneth go to the village where your mother was born. This place holds many memories of that side of the family. While there, you two need to collect sand from her grave. The earth and ground where she was laid to rest have to be involved in this too. You need to bring alcohol as a traditional offering to honor her spirit as well. When you arrive in the village, they will perform a ritual to call your mother's spirit back to her childhood home."

I knew that if I were to stand by her grave, among the memories of our family, this would surely make me feel both respectful and anxious. Every detail of this journey felt important and heavy with tradition.

"John, I promised to protect you from facing unfamiliar customs and strangers. I think if I reach out to another relative, Limbou, who lives in Guinea-Bissau, they might be able to help. Limbou can ask for clarity and more understanding of the situation." My father hoped this would help bridge the gap with our mother's family regarding the complexities of our cultural heritage.

After contacting our relative, my father diligently worked to arrange a meeting, one that would provide insight into everyone's perspectives, concerns, and the family dynamics at play. His effort to facilitate this connection was not only about addressing my fears but also about honoring our heritage and fostering a sense of unity.

I picked up the phone and dialed my sister's number, a knot of anxiety forming in my stomach as I shared the troubling news about our relatives' expectations regarding our mother's memorial.

"My brother," she said, her frustration palpable, "these people have always harbored negative feelings toward our mother. They could not be bothered to even show their faces at her funeral. Now that you are planning to honor her memory with a tribute, you can be sure they will do everything in their power to undermine you."

Her words struck me like a blow. The thought of facing opposition during such a heartfelt endeavor was demoralizing, and I honestly did not know what their grievances or issues were. I felt adrift in a sea of unexpected chaos, overwhelmed and uncertain. But I made a conscious decision to trust my sister's judgment; she had tiptoed around members of this side of the family for more years than I had, and she possessed a deeper understanding of the complexities involved.

Next, I had a video call with my aunt Tani. I explained the troubling circumstances surrounding my mother's memorial—how it had become a battleground for conflicting opinions and demands from family members. I made it clear that I would not succumb to their pressure or give in to their unreasonable requests. This was about honoring my mother's legacy, and I was determined to do so on my own terms.

Aunt Tani listened intently, her brow furrowed with concern, and she firmly advised me against succumbing to their requests. She strengthened my conviction that I should steer clear of the daunting journey to my mother's village to fulfill her relatives' spiritual demands.

Weeks later, the meeting between Limbou and Jokin unravelled into disappointment. My mother's family doubled down and presented a series of even more complicated demands that felt like a tug-of-war, testing the boundaries of our traditions.

Again, they insisted that my sister and I travel to the village to formally announce the intentions regarding our mother's traditional memorial. This requirement now struck me as less of a tribute and more of an insistence on recognition, overshadowing the gravity of our loss. They proclaimed that a specific ritual was necessary to summon my mother's spirit back to her birthplace. While this tradition held deep meaning for them, their expectations felt both significant and daunting at the same time, leaving me grappling with a sense of obligation that conflicted with my desire to honor my mother's memory in my own way.

Their newest demand, however, revealed something unsettling. They claimed my mother had once given birth to a child—referring to me—and had entrusted that child to others, namely my grandparents Baba and Nteh. This was a strong hint that family obligations were unfulfilled. They brought up a troubling story that suggested my grandfather, my mother's father, had placed a curse on my mother before he died. They stated that not only would they not attend the memorial until we promised to perform further rituals, but they also claimed that the curse placed on my mother by her father was too serious to ignore. This weighed heavily on me.

My father then spoke on the phone with Limbou. After having spent some time with my mother's side of the family, Limbou expressed discomfort and suggested there might be issues much deeper than we even knew about. My father and Limbou both agreed that I should cancel my plans for the traditional memorial.

I let my sister and other family members know that I had already told key people about my plan to celebrate my mother's life and honor her memory. In the end, I decided to go ahead with my plans to return home to The Gambia and hold a service for her, especially since the date would mark three years since her passing.

As my departure neared, anxiety mixed with thoughts about my mother's untold story ran through me. The bits of information and the complicated family dynamics from our conversations showed me how little I knew about her background. Even after her death, her full story remained a mystery.

CHAPTER NINETEEN

For my mother's memorial celebration, I eventually settled on a much simpler version of the traditional one I had originally wanted. A few days before my departure from Denver to the sun-drenched shores of The Gambia, I sat across from my father in his living room. Family photographs adorned the walls and shelves, whispering stories of the past.

In many African cultures, probing parents about their past or the nuances of their personal relationships felt forbidden, a delicate subject that children were often discouraged from exploring. But I needed answers.

"Father, please tell me more about Mother," I asked nervously.

To my astonishment, my father exuded a sense of delight, as if I had opened a door to a treasure trove. His warm smile and animated gestures invited me into a conversation that felt both significant and intimate. "I believe that you are finally at the age of understanding—ready to absorb the tales of her life and spirit."

I was heartened by my father's willingness to recount the stories that had long been left untold. He urged me to ask him questions, genuinely curious about what I wanted to learn.

With that encouragement, I took a deep breath and prepared to delve into my mother's life, eager to uncover the pieces of her story that would connect me to my roots and shape my understanding of who she was. "I know that those of us who were close to her were acutely aware of the struggles she faced."

He nodded in agreement.

"What were the underlying reasons for her excessive reliance on alcohol and her unpredictable behaviors that left us all bewildered?"

"Son, I can't pretend to have all the answers, but I am willing to share what I know."

"Your mother was a friend of Juana, and Juana was the one who introduced us."

Juana was a distant cousin of his. During their youth, she had lived with my father, along with my grandparents, for several years, creating a bond between them before she returned to her homeland, Guinea-Bissau. This practice was very common, where a distant relative showed up out of the blue and asked to stay for some time. Juana had a long-standing history with my mother; their paths had crossed again in the vibrant environment of southern Senegal. During their time together, my mother had opened her heart to Juana, revealing her deep yearning to start anew in The Gambia, after her failed marriage.

"So," I interrupted my father's storytelling. "It's true she was married before you?"

"Yes, it seems that way."

"Was this to Neneth's father?"

"Let me start with my story. So, Juana was your mother's friend and reassured her that her brother—me—was living in The Gambia and could offer her shelter." In addition, the possibility of a new relationship hung in the air. Encouraged by Juana and driven by a strong desire for a fresh start, my mother made the bold decision to embark on this journey, following the instructions that would lead her toward an unknown future with hope.

When my mother arrived in The Gambia, her initial excitement turned to confusion as she struggled to locate the exact place Juana had mentioned. The directions she received were vague and unclear. She had been told to ask for my grandfather Baba when she reached the village of Lamin. But Juana had written down Baba's real name, Ndara, on a piece of paper, rather than his nickname. When she got to the Lamin village and asked someone where to find Ndara, she was directed to a different Ndara. As luck would have it, this other Ndara knew my grandfather and father.

The following day, as the sun dipped toward the horizon in the late afternoon, my father and my grandfather were nearly finished plowing the expansive backyard of their family compound.

The rhythmic sound of the plow sliced through the rich, dark soil, revealing the sweet scent of freshly turned earth. Just as they were about to wrap up, they noticed a trio—two men and one woman—making their way toward their home.

The woman stood out; her beauty striking against the backdrop of the rustic compound. Her fair complexion radiated in the sunlight, and her long hair flowed down her back. She exuded an air of confidence that captured the attention of both men. As the guests approached, their footsteps crunched softly on the gravel path.

When the trio reached the porch, my father and grandfather could see the woman start a conversation right away with my grandmother; her voice drifted over the field toward my father's ears. My grandfather, pausing to wipe the sweat from his brow, cast a curious glance their way. With a hint of amusement dancing in his eyes, he turned to my father and remarked, "It seems we have visitors."

One of the men, tall and broad-shouldered, walked over with a purposeful demeanor as my father and grandfather finished their agricultural toil. He addressed my grandfather directly. "We are here for you."

Intrigued by the unexpected declaration, my grandfather excused himself. In the brief exchange that followed, he discovered that the enchanting woman had specifically asked for him. After a short yet engaging conversation, he returned to the field, bewilderment swirling in his mind.

As the sun continued its descent, casting long shadows across the freshly plowed earth, my father, with a sense of anticipation, walked toward the porch to greet the guests. After an exchange of polite introductions, he excused himself to take a refreshing shower; the cool water was a welcome relief after a day of hard labor under the sun.

In a moment of candid reflection, my father shared with me that he had wanted desperately to initiate a conversation with the captivating lady but had hesitated, anxious that his father might reprimand him for being overly bold. He chuckled at his youthful apprehension, blissfully unaware that the beautiful woman had come specifically to meet him.

My father recounted, at first glance, everything in their household that evening seemed perfectly ordinary. He initially thought that the woman was just another relative who had come to visit or perhaps stay for a while as she searched for a job. The two men who accompanied her left after a brief chat, leaving her seated in the living room, where she quietly observed the interactions and energy of the family around her.

Three days later, with a mixture of curiosity and trepidation, the woman approached my grandmother, seeking a private conversation. My father vividly remembered the way his mother relayed this encounter to him in the following days. She had gently asked, "What exactly do you wish to discuss with me?"

The young woman, her voice barely above a whisper,

explained that Juana, her friend known for her kindhearted nature, had urged her to meet my father. Yet, despite her willingness to pursue this connection, she hesitated to reveal the core reason behind her visit, her shyness evident in her downcast eyes.

In those first few days, my father went about his daily routine, still believing that this new guest was a distant relative. On the fourth day, however, his mother delivered an unexpected revelation. The woman was not merely a visitor or a second cousin once removed—she was there for him, sent by a family member to facilitate a deeper connection.

During that time, it was common for men and women to meet through introductions arranged by friends or relatives, akin to a gentle blind date, a social custom steeped in tradition. Surprised by the news, my father felt excitement coupled with anxiety at the thought of engaging with someone he had never met. Yet in his heart, he knew he would remain open, especially since the woman had been recommended by someone he trusted deeply.

Taking on the role of a supportive matchmaker, my grandmother Nteh quickly reached out to the young woman, relaying that my father wanted an introduction.

They all gathered in the cozy warmth of the living room, where a handshake solidified their agreement—a simple yet profound gesture, laden with unspoken hopes and the promise of new beginnings.

My father fondly remembered. "Our initial conversation

felt effortless, as if we had known each other for far longer than just a few days. We shared stories and laughter, each revelation deepening a connection. In an act of kindness, I helped her seek employment, guiding her to a job not far from our family home. This was the start of our beautiful journey together, paving the way for a future full of potential and companionship."

In the time that followed, they settled into a modest yet warm room that fostered a sense of intimacy. She seamlessly integrated into the family's daily life. My father recalled that a year and a half after meeting one another, they married. Shortly after the wedding, they were invited to a lively naming ceremony for his sister's newborn, little Bajen—my aunt. As the family prepared to leave, donning their finest clothes for the celebration, my father remained blissfully unaware that this day would unveil an unsettling truth about my mother.

CHAPTER TWENTY

My mother and father arrived at the already-boisterous party. My father told me when they entered the event, a few of the guests looked at my mother, admiring her natural beauty. She wore a wonderfully tailored dress that flowed gracefully with each movement, and her radiant smile drew everyone's attention.

My father paused his story, lost in the nostalgia of those memories, and said, "John, your mother was an exceptionally pretty woman, captivating and full of life; you would have been amazed." He continued, his voice tinged with affection as he recalled the enchanting young woman who had captured his heart.

At the gathering, men and women sat on opposite sides outside, adhering to the social customs of the day, creating a mosaic of lively conversation and shared laughter. The scents of delicious food and sweet treats filled the air. My father watched my mother as she danced to the music, twirling and laughing. That radiant smile was truly infectious.

Hours later, after the party wound down, they made their way to the bus stop to catch the next one home. Once they boarded, the motion and noise became too much for my mother, and she abruptly began to feel very sick. The bus driver, visibly concerned, instructed my parents to exit, giving them no choice but to wait for another bus to continue their journey home.

It was at that moment, amidst the quiet embarrassment of disembarking the bus, that my father began to understand what was going on. When they eventually arrived home, the house was quiet, with everyone else asleep and unaware. My father gently, yet firmly, asked her, "Did you have anything to drink at the event? Have you ever had alcohol before?"

My mother, her cheeks flushed with shame and regret, offered a heartfelt apology, realizing how her actions had impacted their evening.

As the days turned into weeks, life returned to its tranquil rhythm, and no further incidents suggested that alcohol had entered my mother's habits. One evening, many months after the naming party, while walking back from the farm, my mother joyfully revealed that she was pregnant with me. As my mother's pregnancy progressed, she remained diligent in her work, managing the demands of her job with grace.

Four months after my mother's announcement, my grandfather prepared to host a guest, and he summoned my father to buy some alcohol to ensure a warm welcome. On that particular day, however, my mother still hadn't returned from work, and the minutes stretched into hours, each tick of the clock amplifying anxiety in my father as he awaited her arrival.

My father sat across from me now with a troubled expression. "I waited for your mother as long as possible. I tried to dismiss my worries for a moment and convince myself that she was simply working late. I had been tasked by your grandfather to procure a few bottles of alcohol for the evening. So that was what I set out to do."

As he approached the small, dimly lit storefront, the sight that greeted him shattered his expectations. There was my mother, sitting at a table, laughing softly and holding a drink, even though she was about four months pregnant with me. My father's heart raced, shock and disappointment surging within him. My mother looked up; recognition and shame simultaneously washed over her face. She immediately looked away. Nevertheless, my father managed to retain his composure.

"What did you do?" I asked.

"I went about my purchase. After buying a few bottles, I approached her and Lenny, an old friend who was there too. 'Why don't you both come home with me?' I asked them. But she still couldn't bear to meet my eyes. She was afraid of the disappointment. I again invited them both, hoping to salvage the evening. But she hesitated, her cheeks flushed with humiliation. After a moment's contemplation, she reluctantly agreed to accompany me. Lenny too. As we walked home, the weight of unspoken words hung between us. Then, just outside our compound, your mother stopped, her body stiffening as if struck by an unseen force. 'I can't go in with you,' she declared, and she did this right in front of Lenny. Can you imagine my embarrassment? This moment marked a profound turning point for us, one that I would later identify as the beginning of our relationship's unraveling."

Faced with her defiance, my father felt a mixture of confusion and despair. Rather than push the issue, he decided to honor her wishes and just take the bottles inside to my grandfather, who had been eagerly awaiting his arrival. As he walked away to the front door, more anxiety brewed inside him, and his mind raced at the thought of how to explain my mother's absence to his parents without revealing the painful truth.

After a long period of waiting, and with his concern deepening, my father summoned the courage to venture outside again, retracing his steps back to the junction where he had left my mother and Lenny. To his dismay, neither was to be found. He hurried to Lenny's home, hoping for clarity.

When he arrived, slightly out of breath, Lenny revealed that my mother had returned to her workplace, leaving my father with a heavy heart.

He sprinted to my mother's workplace, but by the time he arrived, the doors were locked, the quiet of the late hour wrapping the house in eerie stillness.

The next morning, she was still missing. So my father rushed back to her workplace. He was met by my mother's boss, whose expression was a mixture of anger and concern. "What did you do to force her to come back here and stay overnight?" she demanded, her voice sharp like a knife cutting through the morning air.

My father responded to this comment with surprising calmness, asking, "Did you ask her what happened?"

The boss recounted how my mother had expressed doubts about my father's stability. Despite my father's earnest attempts to clarify his side of the story, the boss remained displeased, her disapproval clear in her furrowed brow and crossed arms.

After this tense exchange, my mother decided to leave her workplace and sought refuge with another relative who lived nearby in the same village. All the unresolved tensions trailed behind her.

Eventually, my mother relocated to the town of Gunjur. My father, determined to maintain connection, frequently visited, each trip deepening his longing for the family they were starting.

When I was born, it was a well-kept secret; neither my father nor his parents had been informed. It took a serendipitous visit from a family relative, who happened to be in Gunjur on a personal errand, to unveil the news. My mother had welcomed a healthy baby boy into the world.

The moment this news reached my grandparents, joy

erupted in their hearts. They were ecstatic to learn they had a grandson. My father, brimming with nervous excitement, came to see me for the very first time. Later, he returned with his mother Nteh who brought an abundance of gifts, each carefully chosen, overflowing with affection.

As Nteh laid eyes upon her newborn grandson, her heart swelled with emotion, and tears streamed down her cheeks, spilling over with love for her expanding family. That day marked a beautiful new beginning.

My father looked at me from across the living room. "But it was at that moment I knew something was truly amiss with your mother. I couldn't quite grasp the complexities of her behavior or understand the underlying reasons for her actions. But there was a dark cloud hanging over her. What had transformed her into someone I barely recognized? That uncertainty weighed heavily on me, and my mind raced with questions that seemed to have no answers."

His sentence hung in the air as we both sat in comfortable chairs in Colorado, so far away from where my mother's troubling story began and ended.

CHAPTER TWENTY-ONE

A few weeks later, I made my way through the busy corridors of DIA to catch my flight to The Gambia. The thought of reuniting with cherished family and friends for my mother's second ceremony made me excited. Yet the heavy cloud of grief still loomed overhead, reminding me that the purpose of this journey was to honor the memory of my mother.

Upon landing on the sun-kissed shores of my homeland, I immediately remembered the beauty of the rich earth, the vibrant shades of green, and the deep blue sky that seemed to stretch endlessly above. The warm, tropical breeze enveloped me, carrying the distant sounds of laughter and chatter from my welcoming family. They embraced me with open arms, their faces lighting up with both joy and sorrow.

I anticipated the long-awaited conversation with Aunt Tani. And soon, on a tranquil evening, as the sun dipped below the horizon, casting a golden hue across the landscape, my aunt, my sister, and I gathered. We sat in a cozy spot inside a room, surrounded by the sounds of nature. We settled on the bed and floor.

Taking a moment to collect my thoughts, I said, "I am on a quest to uncover the puzzle that is my mother's past."

Aunt Tani, with her warm smile and gentle demeanor, turned to me. "What do you want to know about your mother?"

I wanted to know the events that shaped her experiences, particularly the formative years that had such a profound impact on her adult life. I conveyed the deep importance of revealing her story. It was a narrative that deserved to be told and understood. "I need to know not only for my healing but also to impart lessons and inspire others facing similar challenges."

I was determined to honor my mother's legacy by shedding light on her life, hoping that her experiences would foster empathy for others who struggle.

Aunt Tani began with a deep sigh. "My dear nephew, this is a conversation I never wished to have, but if you insist, we must discuss it." Her voice trembled slightly as she spoke, revealing the emotional turbulence beneath her otherwise calm exterior.

She painted a vivid picture of my mother's life, one that had been permeated by sorrow from the very start. "Your mother was wed at a tender age, thrust into a marriage with a man she did not love. This union was not born of desire or choice but rather the result of our father's unyielding authority and carefully laid-out plans. He had deemed it necessary for her to accept this fate, and she felt she had no avenue for rebellion, as doing so would invite harsh punishment."

Forced marriage has deep historical roots in The Gambia and throughout other parts of Africa. The practice is common in rural areas, where girls are removed from their families and their schools, thus denying them an education and financial freedom, and forcing them into wedlock. Oftentimes, these marriages are not based on love or mutual attraction. What's more, the girls in forced marriages are married to much older men, older by at least ten years.

As Tani spoke, she conveyed the oppression of those early years. She told me about the confinement of their dreams and the extinguishing of hope. This oppressiveness in their childhood and early adulthood lingered like a ghost and shrouded my mother in persistent sadness and insecurity.

My aunt recalled the troubling events of my mother's traditional wedding day, an occasion she and my sister believed left a permanent scar on my mother's spirit. According to the cherished customs of our culture, the members of my maternal grandmother's family were expected to participate, symbolizing the unity and blessings of both sides.

However, a rift emerged when my grandfather obstinately declared that his former in-laws would not take part in the festivities. He insisted that his current wife—my mother's stepmother—would fulfill that role instead of my mother's biological mother, as my grandmother was seriously ill and unable to be present.

"What exactly was the reason behind your mother's absence from the marriage ceremony?" I asked.

My aunt fell silent for a moment, her expression laden with sorrow as tears welled in her eyes. She took a deep breath before sharing the painful reality. Their mother struggled with epilepsy, a condition that sporadically seized her mind and body. In addition, she was prone to losing her sense of direction and would often wander off to the point where no one could find her. Over time, the family grew increasingly concerned for her safety, as her unpredictable episodes could lead her into perilous situations. As a result, it became imperative to keep a vigilant eye on her to prevent her from getting lost in the world around her.

My aunt recounted a haunting memory from her own childhood—when she was just two years old, her mother's illness created an insurmountable barrier to proper care. In a heart-wrenching decision dictated by the need for stability and safety, she was taken away from her mother, who could no longer provide a secure environment. This separation forced my aunt into the unfamiliar arms of another caregiver, leaving behind the warm, nurturing embrace of her own mother, which she longed for deeply.

My grandfather's unexpected decision about who should be at the wedding was not merely a logistical choice; it came laden with emotional weight. His stance not only disregarded tradition but also diminished my mother's connection to her roots, creating an atmosphere of tension and disappointment.

Aunt Tani continued. "Tradition plays a pivotal role in our family's understanding of weddings, holding a deep sense of respect and expectation around the events. According to our customs, it was imperative that your mother's maternal family engage in the ceremony for it to be regarded as legitimate and sacred. This encompassed a series of planned rituals, each having cultural significance—invocations that honor our ancestors, blessings for the couple, and symbolic acts meant to ensure prosperity and harmony in their new life together."

But on the day of the wedding, unexpected tension swept through the gathering when my mother's stepmother appeared. My grandmother's side of the family, already feeling slighted and unacknowledged, abruptly got up and left. Their departure was like a sudden storm cloud overshadowing what should have been a joyous occasion. In the midst of this chaos, my grandfather made the contentious decision to forge ahead with the ceremony, dismissing the traditional protocols that had long been established.

As the ceremony began, the absence of my grandmother's family cast a shadow over the celebration, leaving my mother feeling isolated and unsupported on her wedding day. The emotional ramifications would echo within her long after the last guests departed.

My grandfather's decision came with heavy consequences. Many believed that the wedding, held without the essential rites and blessings of my mother's maternal family, cast a shadow over the union. It was whispered that the spiritual repercussions could leave my mother feeling unmoored, as if the sacred bond of her wedding was compromised, creating a lingering uneasiness and vulnerability in her new journey as a wife.

During her marriage, my mother grappled with the devastating reality of being unable to conceive children with the husband chosen for her by her family. This inability cast another dark shadow over her life. The couple lived in a quiet house, where laughter and the joy of parenthood remained frustratingly out of reach.

A couple of years later, my mother's uncle, a figure of authority within the family, approached her husband and bluntly stated, "Since your wife cannot give you a child, we are taking her away."

With little hesitation, the decision was made to remove her from the marriage, thrusting her into a world of uncertainty and more emotional turmoil.

"Wait. What? She was just taken? What did her husband say when he was told this? Did he fight for her?"

"John, sadly, during this era, such circumstances were commonplace. It was just what was done. The reality of our times back then." Aunt Tani explained how this custom was steeped in tradition and societal expectations. These norms often left men feeling powerless, as they dutifully complied with the wishes of their families, even when it meant sacrificing their own happiness and the well-being of those they loved. It was a poignant reminder of the relentless grip of tradition, often at the cost of personal wishes and freedoms.

Eventually, my mother made the difficult decision to relocate to a different town in Senegal, driven by the need to find work and rebuild her life. It was there that she met the man who would become Neneth's father, forging what she hoped would be a fresh start. By that time, however, she had already endured tremendous loss; her beloved mother had passed away, leaving a void that weighed on her heart. Compounding her grief, she struggled to connect with her father, who seemed increasingly distant and unapproachable during this challenging period.

This is when my mother began to turn to alcohol for comfort. Aunt Tani said, "I cannot tell you the exact moment this transition occurred, because I am not sure of it myself, but I suspect it was shortly after the painful end of her marriage, coupled with the profound sorrow of losing our mother. She faced intense stress from witnessing our mother's illness and her forced marriage. It all seemed to push her toward the bottle as a means of escape."

Aunt Tani also held a belief that was not uncommon in the community—that someone might have bewitched my mother. This suspicion wasn't unfounded; rumors of dark magic and malevolent influences were whispered among neighbors. The idea that external forces exacerbated my mother's hardships added another layer of complexity to the situation, further entrenching my mother in a cycle of excessive drinking.

Aunt Tani then recounted a haunting chapter from our family's past, revolving around my mother's sudden and mysterious departure from home. After vanishing, her father, immersed in anguish and betrayal, issued a proclamation. He placed a curse on my mother, a potent spell woven from his despair and fury. With fierce intensity, he commanded every family member to refrain from seeking her out, warning that anyone who dared to defy his wishes would face dire misfortune. This curse spread through the family like an insidious fire, instilling a profound fear that held everyone captive for years.

Each family member was too afraid to break the silence. The belief in the curse was so ingrained that no one from her father's side even considered the possibility of searching for her until after her passing—until her life reached its tragic end. Except for one brave soul. Her uncle's son. Driven by loyalty and a quest for truth, this cousin dared to confront the suffocating grip of the familial taboo, risking everything.

When my mother passed away, the air was thick with grief. Her funeral was that of profound loss, yet it was overshadowed by the absence of her father's family, who chose not to attend. The only representative from that side was this distant cousin, a solitary figure in a sea of mourners, his demeanor strikingly indifferent to the deep sorrow surrounding him. Phone camera clutched tightly in his hands, in a chillingly casual tone, he had remarked, "I will show my family that she was buried properly and not like a dog, as they had thought."

CHAPTER TWENTY-TWO

It wasn't until I delved deeper into my mother's past that I began to uncover the profound and enduring effects of the traumatic events that shaped her early years. I discovered the troubling and often hidden depths of my mother's suffering, endured at the hands of those who were supposed to be her loving protectors. The pain she experienced throughout her life was not merely heartbreaking; it was a haunting testament to the devastating effects of neglect and betrayal. Her childhood was riddled with adversities—loss of loved ones, a chaotic home environment, and emotional neglect, which left deep emotional scars. These formative experiences shaped her perspectives and influenced the way she interacted with herself and others, leaving her feeling isolated and vulnerable in a world that often felt overwhelming. She had silent battles and was on a constant quest for acceptance and understanding in a world that often turned its back on her.

I found myself haunted by the question of what could

have possibly given rise to such intense hatred within her father's family. Was it solely due to my grandmother's illness, which rendered her incapable of defending her daughter during crucial moments? Or were there deeper, unresolved conflicts, perhaps events or disputes that transpired even before?

Each contemplation led me further down an emotional labyrinth, uncovering layers of familial estrangement that only intensified the ache of my mother's absence. My mother did not deserve the life she endured—a life marked by hardship and heartache.

Even now, a profound sense of sorrow envelops me as I think back on her challenging beginnings; the echoes of her struggles still live in my heart. From a young age, she faced overwhelming challenges, and her experiences became a heavy burden she carried until her final breath.

My mother's experience powerfully illustrates the reality of alcoholism, where there is no adequate support for recovery. Throughout her battle with alcohol addiction, she often felt like a ship lost at sea, struggling to find the help she desperately needed for recovery. Each attempt to seek assistance was met with barriers—unsuitable treatment options or simply a lack of understanding from those around her, plunging her deeper into a painful cycle of dependence that felt inescapable.

In my heartfelt yet misguided attempts to help her break free from the suffocating grasp of alcohol, I unintentionally worsened her condition. The withdrawal symptoms she endured were nothing short of torturous—intense tremors, debilitating nausea, and profound anxiety that left her feeling vulnerable and exposed to hostility. I watched as she battled the physical and emotional pain that accompanied her efforts to quit, often collapsing into despair at the slightest setback.

Looking back on those days, where every exchange with my mother felt like walking on eggshells, I still grapple with the haunting choices we faced. There were moments when the temptation to allow her to continue drinking felt stronger, a seemingly easier path that would spare us from the storm of her attempts at sobriety. Yet, managing her erratic behavior felt like walking through a treacherous minefield. Each day unfolded like a rollercoaster ride, swinging wildly between glimmers of hope and the despair that followed.

The enormity of her struggles, especially with addiction and withdrawal, still weighs heavily on my heart; I felt overwhelmed at the time, like a bystander in a tragic play, faced with the urgency to save her while feeling utterly lost in how to provide the right support. Our community, rife with its own limitations, lacked essential resources and facilities—such as counseling services, support groups, or rehabilitation programs—that could have made a significant difference in her recovery journey. This void left us both feeling isolated and abandoned, as if we were in a storm without a lighthouse to guide us home.

I pondered the nature of her first marriage, which seemed to crush her spirit rather than uplift it. As a young woman, she appeared trapped in a relationship that offered little support or love. Was there hidden abuse that she never spoke of, a darkness that tainted those early years? These thoughts linger, filling my mind with an array of more unresolved questions.

I am regretful, weighed down by the haunting awareness of my failure to truly understand and support her in her time of need. I was ill-equipped, blinded by my limited perspectives, and unable to see the full spectrum of her struggles. The intricate web of her deep-seated issues lay concealed beneath her brave façade.

My mother's story is a profound testament to the myriad of struggles that countless young girls around the world endure, weaving a narrative that is both heart-wrenching and illuminating. It captures not just the challenges she faced but also the strength she mustered to overcome them, highlighting the stark realities of a time and circumstances that are often unacknowledged.

Through sharing her experiences, I aspire to shed light on the profound influence a parent's words and actions can wield in shaping the destinies of their children, as well as the rippling effects they have on generations to come.

Within the pages of this book, there are numerous moments and intimate experiences shared between my mother and me that I can't fully express. Each of these moments serves as a vital thread in our relationship, showing the complexities of love and empathy. As I immerse myself in understanding her past—marked by hardship, sacrifice, and silence—I have a deep sense of remorse for not being able to fully comprehend the extent of her struggles and the haunting trauma she valiantly tried to navigate alone.

Her journey is not merely one of survival; it is a powerful narrative woven with resilience and courage, illuminating the silent battles that many individuals fight in the shadows of their lives. There were times when I felt overwhelmed with a profound and unrelenting anger toward her, convinced that her choice to drink was driven by spite or an insatiable urge to escape her reality.

In the stillness of my thoughts, I now yearn for her presence, wishing I could convey my sincere apologies for my misunderstandings. This experience reveals an important lesson for us as children. It is essential to recognize that our parents, too, might exhibit strange or unexpected behaviors, often rooted in their own complex and painful histories. We need to have a deeper sense of patience and compassion for them and strive to uncover the silent battles they fought and continue to fight, and the emotional wounds they carry. By truly understanding their struggles, we can nurture more meaningful connections and foster a spirit of empathy in our own relationships.

EPILOGUE

This heartfelt memoir stands as a tribute to my late mother, Maria Manneh, whose enduring legacy inspires me to champion understanding, compassion, and proactive measures in addressing forced marriage, addiction, and trauma in all their many forms.

Now that I am a husband and a parent, with all the complexities of adulthood, I strive to piece together the fragmented memories of my past, yearning to understand my own experiences and answer more of the elusive questions that linger.

Writing this book has been an incredibly cathartic yet challenging experience, one that tested my resilience and pushed me beyond my emotional boundaries. Yet, it was an irresistible compulsion that drove me to share my story alongside the narrative of my mother. As I immersed myself in my mother's hidden past, I uncovered a puzzle of sorrowful truths that had been obscured in the shadows of family history and tradition. Each revelation brought both pain and understanding, and through this process, I ultimately found the closure and peace that had eluded me for years.

Exploring my mother's life transformed into an emotional odyssey, deeply affecting my understanding of my own life and relationships. It reshaped my perspective on the fragility of mental health, the often invisible scars people carry, and the crucial importance of compassion and awareness.

The lessons drawn from her life have ignited my passionate commitment to foster a more profound understanding of mental health issues. I aim to shed light on the emotional battles faced by individuals grappling with depression, anxiety, and social withdrawal. As a human community, we have a moral responsibility to extend our hands and hearts to those who feel helpless and vulnerable, ensuring that no one has to endure their suffering in silence. By facilitating dialogue and empathy, we can build a supportive environment where understanding flourishes, allowing everyone to embark on their journey of healing with dignity and care.

I am committed to advocating for individuals around the globe who are contending with the profound challenges of withdrawal, with a particular emphasis on the African continent, where resources and support systems are alarmingly inadequate. Many individuals deal with societal pressures, including the pervasive stigma associated with addiction, the harsh realities of financial instability, and the intricate, often strained dynamics of their social relationships, all of which can exacerbate their struggles and hinder their recovery.

Throughout my personal journey of understanding mental health, I have come to recognize the role that seeking help plays in overcoming these obstacles. This can take many forms, from professional interventions provided by trained therapists and counselors to the more informal yet equally impactful support found within community networks that foster empathy and solidarity. It is crucial that we cultivate a compassionate environment, one that encourages dialogue and understanding, so that those in need feel empowered to reach out for help.

I have invested a considerable amount of time in researching withdrawal symptoms. This has afforded me valuable insight into the intricate and multifaceted nature of addiction and the recovery journey, illuminating the reality that each person's experience is shaped by a complex interplay of personal history, environment, and emotional resilience.

I have learned that seeking professional assistance through avenues such as therapy, medical supervision, and support groups is crucial for a successful recovery. The importance of a nurturing and compassionate network of family and friends cannot be overstated. Emotional support—characterized by genuine empathy, understanding, and a willingness to listen without judgment—serves as a cornerstone for those navigating this challenging path. The presence of loved ones can create a vital safe haven, enabling individuals to express their fears and struggles openly. Such a supportive environment not only fosters healing but also reinforces the idea that they are not alone in their fight against addiction, which can be immensely empowering during such difficult times.

While my mother is no longer physically present, looking back on her life offers me a sense of connection to her. I hold deep gratitude for the short time I had with my mother—a time that has left an indelible mark on my heart. Despite her struggles, she radiated a sense of goodness that was evident to everyone around her. Often, she bore the weight of her suffering in silence, grappling with an inner turmoil that felt insurmountable. Yet, her quiet resilience was hiding a spirit that craved understanding and connection. Her memory is a treasured flame that flickers within our hearts, inspiring us to think about her strength and grace, even with all her struggles. I want her story to resonate with others as deeply as it has with me.

The absence of a close relationship with my mother—a bond that could have flourished but instead became strained due to circumstances beyond her control—has cast a long shadow over my own life. This reality has not just been painful; it has been a heavy burden that I have carried. It serves as a poignant reminder of the deep emotional toll that results when communication breaks down and understanding falters.

I managed to survive the overwhelming pain, despair, and depression that accompanied my journey. God has been my guiding light during the darkest moments, illuminating my path and infusing me with strength and hope when I needed it the most. In addition to my faith, I turned to a variety of other coping mechanisms—music, singing with a choir, exercise, journaling, meditation, and connecting with supportive friends and family—each of which played a huge role in my healing process. These practices not only provided me with solace but also empowered me to reclaim myself during the chaos that life presented. I gradually forged a path toward healing and resilience, discovering strength I didn't know I possessed, a remarkable sense of mental clarity and emotional resilience.

However, despite my earnest endeavors to heal, the haunting specters of past trauma are ever-present, casting a shadow over my interpersonal relationships. Each time I witness mothers embracing their children, their affectionate smiles of unconditional love and care, I can't help but feel a sharp pang of jealousy. These poignant moments spark a tumult of emotions within me, awakening feelings of inadequacy and longing. Healing from generational trauma is a process that takes time and commitment, but I am proud to be on the right path and can genuinely say I feel a remarkable sense of improvement, especially since writing this book.

Immersing myself in this creative process has ignited a profound transformation within me, offering a unique opportunity to explore the depths of my experiences and emotions. Throughout this enriching journey, I have unearthed profound insights into resilience and self-acceptance, learning to recognize the incredible strength that lies in embracing my vulnerabilities instead of shying away from them. Each challenge I faced in my past—whether it was dealing with difficult relationships, overcoming self-doubt, or reconciling past mistakes—has contributed significantly to reshaping my perspective on life.

This process has illuminated the vital role I play as a parent, helping me to understand how my actions and attitudes can influence my children's lives, guiding them as they go on their paths. My commitment to growth has not only transformed me but has also equipped me to be a more compassionate and mindful parent.

I want to create a nurturing and loving environment, a safe haven where my children can flourish. I envision this space with warmth and encouragement, allowing them their unique journeys toward self-discovery and purpose as they go through life. Each day, I strive to embody positivity and resilience, demonstrating the qualities I wish to see develop within them. I aim to guide them toward becoming compassionate, empathetic individuals who can withstand life's trials with grace.

I would like to take a moment to extend my heartfelt thanks to each person who has invested their time in reading my book; your support is invaluable and means more to me than I can express. I encourage you to share my mother's story. Together, let us honor her life by acknowledging the formidable challenges she faced while also celebrating the quiet beauty that blossomed even in the depths of her pain and sorrow. Her experience can educate and inspire us all, prompting a collective duty to advocate for those in need.

Every day without action is another day that the cycle of trauma continues. The urgency is real. So is the possibility of change. I am proof.

Dear parents reading this book: It is essential to grasp the profound impact your actions and decisions can have on shaping your children's lives. Your choices significantly influence their emotional and psychological development, leading to outcomes that can enhance their well-being or inflict lasting harm.

Consider my mother's deeply personal story, which starkly illustrates the effects of her father's erratic and harmful behavior. His outbursts created an unstable home, leaving her with lasting emotional wounds that made it difficult for her to trust others or form healthy relationships. This cycle of pain and dysfunction echoed throughout our family, influencing not just her life, but also the lives of her children and grandchildren, perpetuating a legacy of struggle that we are still working to overcome. This example serves as a reminder of the far-reaching implications of parental influence; our smallest decisions reverberate through time, shaping the emotional fabric of future generations.

As parents, we embrace the responsibility of cultivating

an environment that is not only nurturing and supportive but also vibrant with unconditional love and deep understanding. It is essential to actively engage with our children in meaningful ways—whether through heartfelt conversations during family meals, shared laughter during playtime, or attentive listening during their moments of vulnerability. This creates a dynamic atmosphere where open communication blossoms, empowering our children to explore their unique abilities and passions without fear of judgment.

By dismantling harmful cycles and negative patterns that may have been passed down through generations, we can pave the way for a future brimming with hope, compassion, and resilience. We equip our children with the tools they need to go through life's challenges, teaching them to cultivate empathy and strength as they encounter obstacles. Together, we can foster an enduring legacy of positivity and growth, allowing our children to flourish as confident individuals ready to contribute to the world around them.

Equip your children with a diverse range of skills—academic, emotional, social, and ethical—that will empower them to face the complexities of the world with confidence and grace. Instill in them core values such as empathy, resilience, and integrity, which will serve as their moral compass in both personal and professional spheres. By nurturing these qualities, you are not just preparing them for a successful future; you are also inspiring them to become active and compassionate members of their communities.

Encourage their curiosity and critical thinking, allowing them to pursue their passions and develop a sense of purpose that motivates them to make impactful contributions to society.

As they grow, they will have the opportunity to create a ripple effect of positive change, touching the lives of those around them and influencing the world in meaningful ways. Remember, the legacy we cultivate today—rooted in love, guidance, and empowerment—will last across generations, shaping a brighter and more hopeful future for all.

Dear children reading this book: It is vital to hold your parents in high regard, embrace their guidance with an open heart, and earnestly seek their blessings. My grandfather often imparted a meaningful saying that still rings true: "I can see many miles ahead while sitting, but you, as a child, cannot even see while standing." This statement encapsulates the richness of life experience and the profound wisdom that accumulates over the years. This is a reminder that our parents, having traversed the pathways of life—with all its trials, joys, and insights—are often beyond our youthful understanding. The parent-child bond enables us to experience the world through their unique lens, emphasizing the richness of diverse experiences and the lessons that time bestows upon us. So, take a moment to listen closely and value what they share; their insights may guide you through challenges and enrich your journey in ways you have yet to imagine.

By engaging in sincere conversations and absorbing their

compelling stories and thoughtful advice, we deepen our understanding and appreciation for the hard-earned wisdom that has been shaped through years of trials and triumphs. Embracing their insights allows us to think about our own lives with greater clarity and intention, while simultaneously fostering a profound connection with them.

As you reach the end of this book, I encourage you to take a thoughtful moment to delve into the relationships that have left a lasting imprint on your life. Reflect on the individuals whose influence has not only molded your character but also tested your resolve during challenging times and inspired your personal growth. Picture the medley of connections you have nurtured along the way—whether it be the support and unconditional love of your family, the laughter and shared experiences with friends who have stood by you, or the insights and guidance from mentors who have illuminated your path. Each of these relationships has contributed unique lessons and shaped the person you have become. Allow yourself to appreciate the roles they have played in your life. Recognizing how each bond has added depth to your story and resilience to your spirit.

Now is the perfect time to reach out to someone you care about. Consider initiating a heartfelt conversation, perhaps over a cozy cup of coffee or during a leisurely walk in the park, where you can openly share your thoughts and emotions with sincerity and vulnerability. If words feel overwhelming, you might prefer to simply engage in activities that bring you joy—playing a favorite game, watching a movie, or exploring new places together—creating beautiful memories in the process. By prioritizing and nurturing these vital connections, we not only strengthen the bonds but also foster the kind of supportive, healthy communities where everyone thrives.

Ultimately, this commitment to connection can lead to a more compassionate and interconnected world, where understanding and kindness flow freely among us all. Embrace this opportunity to deepen your relationships and spread warmth to those around you.

Let my narrative serve as a reminder of the strength that love can provide, even in the most daunting times. As you go on your own journey of self-discovery, with twists and turns and moments of introspection, I encourage you to embrace and celebrate the mosaic of the diverse stories that define your life.

Together, let us dedicate ourselves to nurturing and deepening our relationships with those who bring richness, joy, understanding, and support. Though my cherished mother has left this world, her spirit and essence remain vividly alive, and memories of her are forever etched in the hearts of those she so lovingly touched.

ABOUT THE AUTHOR

John Manneh was born and raised in The Gambia. In 2010, he completed a two-year program in Architectural Draftsmanship from the Gambia Technical Institute and worked in the construction industry. He moved to the United States in 2014 and has been working with the Regional Transportation District in Denver, Colorado. John enjoys spending time with his wife, children, and relatives. He loves football (soccer), going to the gym, watching movies and shows, and taking walks while listening to music.